Start and Run a
Bed&Breakfast

All you need to know to make money from your dream property

LOUISE & DAVID WESTON

Second Edition

howtobooks / **smallbusinessstart-ups**

Published by How To Books Ltd
Spring Hill House, Spring Hill Road,
Begbroke, Oxford OX5 1RX, United Kingdom
Tel: (01865) 375794 Fax: (01865) 379162
info@howtobooks.co.uk
www.howtobooks.co.uk

How To Books greatly reduce the carbon footprint of their books by sourcing their typesetting and
printing in the UK.

First published 2006
Reprinted 2007, 2008
Second edition 2011

British Library Cataloguing in Publication Data A catalogue record for this book is available from the
British Library.

ISBN: 978 1 84528 443 5

Produced for How To Books by Deer Park Productions, Tavistock
Typeset by specialist publishing services ltd, Montgomery
Printed and bound in Great Britain by Bell & Bain Ltd, Glasgow

Note: The material contained in this book is set out in good faith for general guidance and no liability
can be accepted for loss or expense incurred as a result of relying in particular circumstances on
statements made in the book. The laws and regulations are complex and liable to change, and readers
should check the current position with the relevant authorities before making personal arrangements.

Start and Run a
Bed&Breakfast

Well thought out and well written. A pleasure to read and plenty to think about. – **R.R.**

A gem of a book, it really has given me everything and more to help me make my venture the success I hope it will be. – **D.F.**

I am very happy … I have found information that is very useful to me and am only half way through your book … well worth buying. – **S.K.**

Very useful and just what I was looking for. An invaluable guide. – **P.B.**

It is indeed a jungle out there with all the rules and regulations … I thoroughly enjoyed and was horrified by your book in equal measure, and in some parts if I wasn't so determined to start, I might have dropped out! Most of all it was extremely useful and a good benchmark. – **A.S.**

Exactly the kind of book I was after. My wife and I have longed to start a B&B and move into a farmhouse. Your book will prove such a useful resource, I'm very impressed with it – it's clear and concise. – **S.T.**

I enjoyed your book and some of your tips have been really useful. I have only been in this business for a year and one thing that really boosted my confidence was your point that being individual can be an advantage so I'm now developing my own 'style' of hospitality, instead of trying to be like, for instance, a small hotel chain. – **J.M.**

We read it in February 2007 when we took over running our B&B in the Lake District. Never looked back. The book was invaluable!!! – **T.W.**

Very interesting and informative … it has given me a lot of food for thought, in fact I found it so interesting I read it from cover to cover in about two days. – **S.R.**

Full of good comments and advice in an easy to read format … it will be re-read many times in the future months and will be a very useful reference to get us started. – **S.H.**

The book filled me with enthusiasm and also opened my eyes to what goes on behind the scenes. The most helpful was working out how to price and book rooms and the red tape of rules and regulations. – **L.W.**

The book is first class and has given us a real insight to all aspects of this type of business. We are still at the stage of researching B&B as a means of investing for our future and your book really does answer all our questions – and we are still not put off! – **D.F.**

I have read the book through from cover to cover and have found it very informative. The bit that sticks in my mind is the budgeting, it was really interesting and the exercises gave me food for thought. – **L.L.**

Fantastically helpful and full of really practical advice. – **D.A.**

CONTENTS

Part Two: Running your B&B

INTRODUCTION TO THE FIRST EDITION

Like many people (including you, as you have picked up this book), we had toyed vaguely on and off over the years with the idea of opening a B&B. It seemed a good way of financing and 'justifying' a beautiful house in an attractive location. But we never did anything about it – until, for job reasons, we found ourselves having to move from our long-time Sussex home to the unspoilt little abbey town of Sherborne in deepest rural Dorset.

We ended up buying a 300-year-old house whose 21 rooms and 4,000 square feet were more space than our family of four needed. We had two or three spare bedrooms and, as the house had recently been a hotel and restaurant, they were all en-suite. Now, if ever, was the time to put our pipe dreams into practice – and we did.

We learned a lot in our first year, and more in our second, and much of it the 'hard' way. We wished that we had started with the benefit of a practical guidebook based on hands-on experience, so that we could learn from others' mistakes rather than having to repeat them ourselves. Now we have written that book, and this is it.

When we set out to become B&B hosts, we had never done it before, and had all sorts of worries and doubts. Would we find our way through all the confusing and conflicting red tape and regulations? Would we make enough money to justify the work, and help pay for the house? How much work would it involve, and would we cope? How would it affect our family life? What would it be like having a succession of strangers in our own home? Would they be friendly, or over-demanding? If you are considering opening a B&B for the first time, you must have a similar list of anxieties.

One of our aims in this book is to answer those questions and allay those doubts. And because we started recently enough to remember 'day one' as B&B virgins, we have tried to write the book that we would have wanted then. It is too late for us to avoid the pitfalls and mistakes we made – but, if you have bought this book, we will guide you through the minefields using the personal experience we have picked up.

One question is worth answering right now, before we get going with Chapter 1: you are probably wondering whether the experience has lived up to our initial hopes and expectations. Has it been worth it, after all? Would we, knowing what we now know about the day-to-day reality of running a B&B, recommend it? The answer is yes. We have helped finance the house we wanted, in a place people from around the world choose to visit for its beauty. We have met lots of interesting people, most of whom tell us they envy us our home and our home town. Yes, we have had problems, and it can be hard work at times – especially if your lack of inside knowledge and experience makes it harder than it needs to be. But it won't be as hard for you – after all, you've got the book we wish we had been able to buy.

INTRODUCTION TO THE SECOND EDITION

We were delighted with the reception this book got from readers – it showed that practical advice based on experience was what most people wanted. It has been reprinted since to meet demand, but enough has changed in the four years or so since the First Edition to justify a completely revised and updated edition – hence the book you are reading now.

What has changed? First, there have been developments in regulations, notably on fire precautions and the fragmented and confusing area of copyright licences. These have been brought up to date in this edition.

Secondly, we contacted over 1,000 readers and asked for their suggestions for additions and improvements to the book and have tried our best to fill in the gaps accordingly. This edition consequently has more on payment, online booking and a few other subjects readers told us they were interested in.

Finally, because David has been immersed in the B&B industry over the last few years, heading up the Bed and Breakfast Association (the award-winning trade association for B&B and guest house owners throughout the UK; see www.BandBassociation.org), he has had a unique insight into what starting and running a B&B in Britain involves and what the rewards – and pitfalls! – are in this £2 billion+ cottage industry of some 30,000 small businesses. What he has learnt since then about the government, local authorities and regulators, and their attitude to very small businesses (and indeed to the tourism industry in general) has, we hope, added further insight into this new edition.

PART ONE
PLANNING AND PREPARATION

1
'THE INDIVIDUAL IS BEAUTIFUL'

B&Bs are one of the glories of the British tourist industry … the antidote to the claustrophobic uniformity of chain hotels. Britain's vast network of B&Bs is something that foreigners envy but appear unable to emulate (*The Times*, 12 June 2008).

Out with hotels, in with B&Bs …
British bed and breakfasts are set for a revival as hotels are now so expensive that most families cannot afford to stay in them (*The Times*, 12 January 2008).

Adam Raphael, editor of the *Good Hotel Guide*, is reported as saying that 'B&Bs offer the best value', and that B&Bs 'offer the best breakfasts in Britain'.

For elegant accommodation, look to the new breed of homely yet stylish British bed and breakfasts (Sally Shalam, *Guardian*, 17 May 2008).

If this trend continues, there will soon be no need for luxury hotels. Designed with flair and confidence, run with painstaking attention to detail and offering the kind of sociable welcome that no hotel could ever match, they are a joy to stay in (Walter F. Stowy, the hotel inspector for *The Sunday Times*, on judging the 'Top 10 B&Bs in England' in April 2005).

What B&B stands for now is 'more bang for your buck' – a room in a new wave B&B is basically as good as, or better than, a hotel room – at half the price (Nikki Tinto of i-escape.com cited in the *Guardian*, 17 May 2008).

Pillows are feather, coffee is Illy, jam is home-made, and breakfast is whenever you want it to be. The British B&B has upped its game (*The Times*, 25 April 2009).

Keeping ahead of the game

You can be ahead of the game in the hospitality industry. After the increasing blandness and uniformity which was a trend of the sixties, seventies and eighties as hotel groups sought to impose consistent corporate styles across branded chains, now the new trend is back to individuality. The buzzwords in hotel group boardrooms are 'uniqueness' and 'personality', and hotels which had been expensively refitted to be exactly the same as their branded counterparts in every other city are now being given a new corporate makeover – to look like individual, unbranded hotels or, at the top of the market, like private houses.

By running a good B&B in your home, you are there already! You can offer real uniqueness, not the spray-on corporate kind. You don't have to pretend to be a quirky, characterful, idiosyncratic private home welcoming guests – that is what you are!

So do remember that one of the reasons people choose a B&B is because they want that personal welcome and those individual touches. Many B&B owners aspire to the status of hotels by copying them: they think that minibars, trouser presses, generic 'hotel décor' and 'hotel style' reception desks will help. In fact, by aping hotels they are throwing away the one biggest advantage B&Bs have, which hotels themselves are now trying to pretend to: individuality.

 Go the extra mile with thoughtful 'extras' – particularly where they cost you next to nothing. A couple of home-made biscuits or a glass of iced water may make more impression on your guest than that designer wallpaper that cost you thousands.

The trick is to get the balance right: clients appreciate character and individuality, but also have some non-negotiable areas of expectation. Private en-suite bathrooms are one example: no amount of character will make up for having to walk down a corridor in the middle of the night for a pee. And 'quirkiness' has its limits too: a witty theme to the décor is good, but bizarre or disturbing 'art' or uncomfortable furniture (however stylish) is not going to encourage recommendation or return visits.

The great B&B revolution

For elegant accommodation, look to the new breed of homely yet stylish British bed and breakfasts says **Sally Shalam**.

Champion of the individual B&B and creator of the Special Places guidebooks Alastair Sawday says: 'If you pay £90 for a B&B for two, you will get all sorts of little extras: conversation, views, peace, breakfasts to remember, advice and even help when needed. And all this from delightful human beings rather than corporate functionaries. For the same £90 a hotel simply cannot do it.'

Nikki Tinto [of trendsetting interned accommodation site i-escape.com] goes even further and ventures to compare modern owners to 'personal concierges' who will give invaluable insights into the local area.

What has happened is that a generation of well-travelled, discerning, often design-literate professionals has decided that urban stress is fine Monday to Friday but at the weekend they deserve a break. As the number of short trips we take increases (up to 10 per year on top of longer holidays), cheap flights to European cities aren't always the answer and Britain, as a consequence, is getting a bigger and bigger slice of the weekend-break pie.

We spent an incredible £1bn staying in B&Bs last year. While holidaying in our own backyard enables us to keep an eye on the carbon footprint, it's not the full story. The fact is, short breaks in Britain are now undeniably hip.

According to VisitBritain, which assesses the lion's share of the accommodation in this country, 41% of it is bed and breakfast. And in my experience, and others', much of it has upped its game.

'The style of accommodation has evolved dramatically,' says Sawday. 'Many bed and breakfasts are offering luxurious elements such as flat-screen televisions, designer furniture and high-quality bedding.'

The AA – celebrating the centenary of its hotel services this year – had to introduce a new category to its annual awards last year to reflect the current change. In addition to its traditional Landlady of the Year (a delightful anachronism worthy of sponsorship by Bryson), an award is now made for the funkiest B&B. The title might sound a bit like your dad trying to sound street but you get their drift. I even hear that adding more categories is currently under discussion.

Owners are part of a new breed of 'landlady' (though many are male, of course). These are often relocating city dwellers looking for a means to diversify or for help with a hefty mortgage. Often without any previous experience in the hospitality industry, many are, in my experience, pulling off the whole show incredibly well.

The most disappointing breakfasts I eat these days are in hotels, while B&Bs repeatedly bring outstanding stuff to my table. There might not be a newspaper outside my door first thing, but it's a small price to pay for freshly squeezed juice and a plate of food cooked to order instead of something that's been kept hot under a grill for half an hour.

The expectation level is notching up so fast that there's no knowing what B&Bs will throw in next. For now though, according to Nikki Tinto, it's acceptable to expect some of these: 'Probably free wireless internet, usually an honesty bar or even a butler's pantry and, when you arrive, you might get afternoon tea with a slice of homemade cake.'

(© Guardian News & Media Ltd 2008)

2
BEFORE YOU START

Who should start a B&B?

Are you the right person to run a B&B? Are you doing this for the right reasons? What are your objectives, and will a B&B enable you to achieve them? These may seem odd questions. If you have bought this book, you are clearly interested – at least in finding out whether you want to run a B&B. We don't want to put you off, but we don't want to encourage you to do something that you would not enjoy, either.

Look at it this way: if reading this book only helps you decide that a B&B is *not* for you, then it's money very well spent (a few of the notes of thanks we received from readers of the first edition were from those who thanked us for helping them decide that running a B&B was *not*, after all, for them). You don't want to find that out after moving and/or investing a lot of money in adapting a property.

So it makes sense to think very carefully about this at the outset.

Are you the right person to run a B&B?

If you never have friends or relations to stay because you can't stand other people in your home, then don't run a B&B! If you don't like meeting people and can't make small talk, then don't run a B&B. You do need to be able to relate to people to do the job – although you *don't* have to be a 'life and soul of the party' type – in fact, if you are, you may irritate as many people as you attract.

ALARM BELL

Don't start in this business at all if you hate dealing with people, can't cope with early starts or if you are lazy, impatient or have a quick temper. Running a B&B is not as back-breaking as trawler fishing or coal mining, but it can involve hard work at unsociable hours and often requires diplomatic charm in the face of extreme provocation.

COPING WITH CLUTTER AND CLEANLINESS

Being a people person is a vital and, of course, fairly obvious requirement for running a hospitality business. But there are less obvious character traits you need too.

If you hate housework with a passion and feel comfortable amid clutter, chaos and congealed crockery from yesterday's dinner, you probably feel that you are admirably liberated from other people's obsessive hang-ups about tidiness or cleanliness. You may be right but, although your tolerance threshold of your own debris may be high, other people's tolerance threshold of your debris will almost certainly be much, much lower – close to zero, in all probability.

The fact is that most people are attracted by a sense of order, tidiness and cleanliness – it feels as if care has been taken to make things welcoming. Most people are put off, even repelled, by strangers' personal clutter and by grubbiness. It gives the opposite impression: that their hosts don't care about making things 'nice' for them.

Of couse, a certain amount of clutter could always be excused as part of the décor – think 'eclectic', 'chintzy' or 'cottage style'. Now, though, guests are much more style conscious and often equate stylishness with minimalism. So there is even less excuse than there ever was for untidiness when you are expecting guests to pay to stay in your home.

ALARM BELL

Don't let the audience see behind the set. Keep the piles of dirty laundry, stacks of unwashed dishes and your stocks of spare loo paper hidden in your 'private' areas, leaving the public areas uncluttered, attractive and welcoming.

If in reading this you feel shocked that people could be so judgemental and think they should chill out more and go with the flow, then our appeal to you is: do be open minded enough to question whether you should run a B&B. You may not be suited to it.

If, however, you take pride in showing your home at its very best at all times and are the sort of person who can't walk by a white thread on a dark carpet without picking it up and binning it, then read on. You have a key quality for B&B ownership!

So liking people and being houseproud are two important characteristics for the ideal B&B owner. There are others, too.

BEING METHODICAL AND KEEPING YOUR TEMPER IN CHECK

If you can't ever manage to keep your diary up to date, often forget appointments and keep losing the post-it notes you leave yourself all over the place as reminders, then do take a long hard look at your organisational skills. If you run a B&B you *must* be very methodical and organised with your diary, record-keeping and scheduling.

One of the worst things you can do is forget a booking, overbook or put it in for the wrong date. Even being out when guests arrive because you forgot their arrival time can lead to serious problems!

Are there any more aspects of your personality to look at? The last one we'd mention is an even temper – or at least the ability to control your temper and keep your emotions from flaring up. Things can get trying at times and, if you are likely to fly into a rage or into floods of tears when provoked, maybe you should not be dealing with the public in your own home.

ALARM BELL

Don't let your negative feelings show, however annoying your guests are (and some will be, believe us). An off-hand word or irritated expression from you can spoil your customer's stay and undo all your planning and hard work.

Pass with flying colours so far? Don't worry, nobody's perfect. The important thing is to think hard whether you really want to take in paying guests. Be honest with yourself. Only you can decide.

Writing your business plan

There is a lot of needless mystique about business plans. If you wish you can buy lengthy and complex books about writing business plans. First, yes, it is very important to have a business plan. Secondly, don't be put off – this all boils down to three things:

1. Putting down in writing a comprehensive plan for your business, with both words and figures, forces you to think through all the key aspects and forces you to quantify your financial expectations and commitments.

2. The written plan is something you can show third parties, such as your bank, should you want to borrow money.

3. The business plan gives you a yardstick to measure your actual performance against.

It is as simple – and as important – as that. The financial sophistication of a business plan depends on 1) the scale and complexity of financial decisions which depend on it; and 2) the number and independence of the parties to your business plan.

NUMBER AND INDEPENDENCE OF THE PARTIES

Taking 2) first, companies floating on the stock exchange ('IPOs' or initial public offerings) have to put together very detailed 'prospectuses' (basically, a business plan for prospective shareholders), because they are dealing with people with no other connection with the business or source of knowledge. It all has to be spelt out, with every option and every caveat. Even smaller, private businesses will have to have a very thorough and detailed business plan if they are new ventures seeking millions from outside investors.

As someone starting a B&B, you will probably be buying the property with your own money (perhaps with the help of a standard property mortgage) – or you may own the property already. You will probably be using it as your home and you will probably not be seeking outside investors. If this description fits you, then many of the most onerous demands of a business plan do not apply to you. The major financial decision – whether or not to buy the property – is in all likelihood separate from the B&B business itself. It has to be said too that, unless you have recklessly overpaid for a property in a declining area, the last 50 years would tell us that over the medium to long term (10 years plus), it is hard not to gain on any investment in property in the UK.

SCALE AND COMPLEXITY

This means that the scale of the financial decision you are taking is relatively modest – the conversion of your property for B&B use and marketing costs – and the major financial commitment you are carrying (i.e. your ownership of the property) is in effect your investment in your own home, and is a safe bet in the long term unless the UK economy suffers a catastrophic setback.

RUNNING A BUSINESS FOR FINANCIAL BENEFIT

All this is to reassure you and to set things in context, but we are *not* saying that your business plan doesn't matter. It does. It all comes back to the word 'business' – are you wanting to run a business, for your financial benefit? If so, the business needs to be properly founded, your assumptions need to stack up and the figures need to add up.

If you are not wanting to run a business but simply want to play at hosting paying guests, without wanting to make money out of it, then don't bother with a business plan. It would be a complete waste of your time. If, however, you are serious in wanting to go into B&B on a commercial basis, for financial gain, then you *must* write a business plan. It does not need to be half an inch thick and full of management speak and multi-coloured graphs, but it does need to be well thought through, using realistic assumptions, and to show exactly how you will achieve your financial expectations, and when, and with what commitment of money and other resources.

WRITING THE PLAN

The basic process of writing a business plan is sheer common sense. Don't be worried or intimidated by management books into thinking that it is beyond you or requires huge expertise or experience. It doesn't. Concentrate on the simple basics, not the form or language:

- ☐ What kind of business am I trying to create?

- ☐ How will I create it?

- ☐ How will I run it and how much will it cost?

- ☐ How much revenue will this bring in?

If you focus on these, and think everything through thoroughly, you should not go wrong.

These four questions are deceptively simple. The answers are crucial and require a lot of careful thought and planning. The following chapters take these one by one.

3
DETERMINING YOUR MARKET

Your location (country, town, seaside), the quality of the décor and rooms, the character of your building and the facilities you can offer will determine what section of the market you should be pitching for. The seasonality of your market is a crucial factor, as is the competition you will be up against.

What kind of business are you trying to create?

As you are reading this book, the short answer would be 'a B&B'. But this is not specific enough to be any use for a business plan. Your answer needs to define what the business books would no doubt call your product offering, positioning and target market. You could just as easily call it the character of your intended B&B and the clientele you believe will be attracted to it.

This needs thought and a good dose of realism: be honest with yourself rather than letting wishful thinking influence you. If you own a 1930s semi two streets back from the seafront of a traditional coastal resort in Ayrshire, for instance, it would not be sensible to expect to command high prices or a long season, or to expect high levels of corporate midweek business out of season.

This is where hard-headed logic, and as much research as you can do (or experience you already have), will be needed. The nature and character of your B&B will be mainly dictated by the character of the property itself and those famous three priorities recited by property investors: location, location, location.

If you have not yet bought your property

If you have not yet bought the property you are thinking of running as a B&B, we strongly advise you to pause, think and do some homework at this stage. It's not too late!

Think about the location and look at the existing competition. Try to find out as much as you can about it. What do the other comparable B&Bs charge? When do they open and close? When are they full? This is a difficult one to find out, but look for 'no vacancies' signs, call with inquiries about availability and try to chat with the owners about business.

Think about the particular location you have in mind. What will most visitors who stay there in B&Bs be coming for? If it is a popular coastal resort, that may bring a ready market and a good long average stay, but the downside may be a short season, with no other sources of business outside the school summer holidays.

ALARM BELL

Don't fall into the trap of competing on price alone. Hotels with dozens of rooms have to fill them in low season somehow but, with only a few rooms, you need good revenue per booking. And if you care for your home, you will not want to fill it with people whose only criterion is cheapness. Life is too short!

Cities will usually give the opposite profile: a much more year-round business, possibly even dipping in high summer, and a much shorter average stay (business people often stay only one night and usually on a single-occupancy basis).

At the coastal resort, your clientele will probably be families or retired couples perhaps, and they will be what the travel industry calls 'leisure travellers' – visiting your area for pleasure, on a holiday or short break. In a city, though, you will also get people staying on business. The proportion of business people will depend on your location and the city. If your B&B is in a picturesque part of Bath, for instance, you will probably attract mainly leisure travellers, but if it is in the business district of Birmingham, you will probably get more business travellers.

This is as much an art as a science, but we can't stress enough how important it is to think through what type of business you want to run and to buy your property accordingly – or, if you already own the property you want to run as a B&B, to be realistic as to the type of business it is suited for.

If you already own the property

This makes life simpler, as your choices are much narrower! Think through the type of property you have (art deco bungalow, thatched cottage or Georgian townhouse?), the size of the rooms, the facilities you have or can create (en-suite bathrooms? swimming pool?) and the style and quality of décor (traditional with antiques? Laura Ashley country chintz? modern and minimalist? clean but basic?). Next, think about your location: what is the mix of visitors? What is the balance of families, couples and singles? Are visitors typically older or younger? Will they be mainly staying on business or for a holiday or break?

Your answers to all these questions need to be weighed up and they will guide or dictate several key business plan decisions.

ROOM DÉCOR AND FACILITIES

Business people want functional comfort, so a desk and Internet access, for instance, may be important, and the décor should be restrained and conservative rather than twee or chintzy. The infamous trouser press may even actually be used! Family holidaymakers will want multi-bedded family rooms and will appreciate things like games consoles and children's videos. A very upmarket clientele will dictate a high spend on furniture, fittings and fabrics, whereas if you will be working at the budget end of the market, you cannot justify this and must limit your spend accordingly. Plan the layout and décor of your rooms with your expected mix of guests in mind.

THE MIX OF ROOM TYPES

Here you are, of course, limited by the number and size of rooms in the building (unless you plan to build an extension). Within these constraints, however, you need to decide which rooms will have an en-suite bathroom (if space allows) and which will become singles, twins, triples or family rooms. Again, plan this with your clientele in mind.

Whatever your clientele, though, don't ever put a single bed in a room that will take a double: put in a double and allow for two as far as fittings are concerned. If you sell it as single occupancy, the guest will appreciate a double bed, but more importantly you can also sell it as a double. If you have small rooms that would not fit a double bed – especially if they would not fit an en-suite bathroom either – then, before making them singles, consider knocking them into the next room to create a family room or suite, or making a spacious bathroom to the next-door bedroom.

YOUR MARKETING STRATEGY

Clearly this must be geared towards generating the type of clientele that suits your B&B (see Chapter 17 on marketing).

If you are still looking for a property

Congratulations, all your options are still open! Rather than having most of your key decisions on rooms, décor and marketing dictated by the property you already have and its location, you can enjoy the freedom to *choose* the type of B&B you want to run first, *then* look for a suitable property and location for that type of business.

In reality if your B&B will be your home as well, this decision will not be a pure business judgement but will be mixed in with (or completely subsidiary to) your personal decision on where you want to live and the lifestyle you want to enjoy. Fair enough – first things first. But your B&B will be a business, so do make an effort to think through the business aspects of your decision. This is especially important if the B&B income is expected to be a major part of your income: if your business will be important to you, then you should treat the early, critical choices with the importance they deserve as business decisions.

Beware: this stage in the planning process is fraught with dangers from a potential enemy who might sabotage your business – yourself! If you will be relying significantly on B&B income to fund your new lifestyle, then you *must* keep a sensible business 'hat' on when weighing up whether to commit yourself to a property. A B&B is a property-based business so the choice of property is everything.

There is no point, for instance, in choosing purely for lifestyle reasons to buy a remote cottage in an unpopulated area, then trying to run a B&B business from it. The same factors which made you choose to live there yourself – the remoteness and lack of people – also make it a disastrous choice for a business which depends on a steady flow of people to the area.

We'd have to ask, in such an example, why do you want to run a B&B at all? If you want to 'get away from it all' – including from people – then don't run a B&B. It's a people business.

Be realistic

You as a businessperson must guard against the insidious arguments you may hear from a very persuasive source – you as a person. Yes, listen to them: why not plan for a business to fund your lifestyle? We did. *But* be realistic: if the business has to fund your lifestyle, then, first, it has to work as a business.

A particular temptation – one of the worst pitfalls in planning any hospitality or tourism business – is to persuade yourself that, because *you* have fallen in love with a place which no one else seems to know or visit, you will be able to persuade others to see the undis-covered attractions of the place and come to stay in your B&B. It seems plausible, after all: 'this place is so lovely, all I have to do is tell people – advertise it – and they will come and fall in love with it as I did'.

No! If this is what you are telling yourself, then the next sentence alone will be worth many times the price of this book. You cannot create a demand for an area on a B&B's marketing budget, you can only capture a share of the existing demand.

Think about your budget

Local and regional tourist offices spend millions of pounds over periods of many years to achieve a marginal increase in visitors. What chance have you got? The sort of budget needed to change people's travelling habits is way beyond what you could viably spend to promote your B&B.

This may seem depressing and defeatist. Nevertheless, it is true. You have been warned! Examining why this is true is worth a detour, as it provides a very fundamental lesson in marketing which may help you in planning to promote your B&B.

Advertising

To reach the undecided and change their behaviour, you have to indulge in very expensive, mass-media, intrusive advertising. TV is the ultimate example. McDonald's and Coca Cola put their branded ads on TV to make their brands enter the consciousness of viewers so that, next time those viewers want a burger or a soft drink, they are more likely to choose the heavily advertised brands rather than their competitors'. That kind of mainstream, high-volume, high-impact advertising – call it 'big' advertising for short – *can* change behaviour and, if you had McDonald's advertising budget, you might have a chance of persuading people who have never heard of you or your area to book a holiday at your B&B.

If you haven't got McDonald's money, however, you can't do 'big' advertising. The good news is that 'small' advertising can be very effective – and for less than the price of one daily Big Mac. Small advertising does the opposite of big – rather than put a new thought into people's minds, it tucks itself away waiting to be found by people who already know where they are going.

An example: people wanting to buy a second-hand car will look in the used-cars section of their local paper. Placing a three- or four-line classified ad there will reach those self-selected readers. The ad will be read by far fewer people than those who see the colour Coca Cola ad on the front cover, but almost all the 50,000 people who see the Coca Cola ad will take no notice of it, whereas all the dozen or so people who actually do read the car ad will be in the market for a car. That's why they're looking there.

So the type of advertising we can do as B&B owners is limited to small – but smart – advertising. Think through all the places where your potential clients will be looking to find somewhere to stay in your area, and try to get a cost-effective presence in the most promising of them there is – more on this later, in Chapter 17 on marketing.

4
BUDGETING

Budgeting sounds a boring subject, but it is vital to do this carefully right from the start: it concentrates your mind on the hard economics and tells you what the potential rewards are and the occupancy you need to achieve them. Your budget will become your main financial management tool.

ALARM BELL

Don't skip this chapter! You might be tempted to yawn at the idea of budgeting, but a vast number of small businesses fail because they get this basic element wrong.

Again, as with business plans, the 'Business and Management' shelves in every bookshop are groaning with fat volumes on budgeting. These are full of impressive and daunting jargon. Yes, there is a science to budgeting, and David had to produce very detailed budgets to convince the venture capitalists and bankers to lend several million pounds for his management buy-out some years ago, but here the 'horses for courses' rule applies: keep things as simple as they can be for the business decision you are making and the number of outside participants.

We will try to cut through to the bare essentials of budgeting which you will require in taking your own decision about your own property, without outside investors.

Using a business model

Let's take that famous business model: running a whelk stall. After all, it is a common accusation against the disorganised that they 'could not run a whelk stall', as if nothing could be simpler. This jibe is typically hurled in Parliament from one political side to the other.

How *do* you successfully run a whelk stall? This seems an odd question, but bear with us.

What is 'success' for the whelk stallowner?

☐ Selling all the whelks?

☐ Selling for the maximum price?

☐ Making the most sales turnover?

Once you think this through, it is clear that not one of these answers is the whole answer. If you sell all your whelks for too low a price, for instance, you may still make a loss. Even if you sell out at a good price, you may make a miserable return if your stall was very expensive to buy in the first place and did not last as long as you had hoped.

Running a whelk stall is Fred's livelihood. He lives on the net return of the whelk stall week-in, week-out, so he measures its success in terms of long-term sustainable profitability. This simple-sounding measurement of success, though, is in practice a complicated mixture of (taking only the basics) the following:

☐ The cost of the stall and equipment (capital costs).

☐ The cost of financing this if you are paying interest on the money (finance costs).

☐ The cost of buying the whelks each morning from the wholesale fish market, and other daily essentials like ice, gas bottles for cooking, polystyrene tubs, condiments etc. (direct costs).

☐ The wages of your stallholder, if you pay anyone (payroll costs – an 'overhead').

☐ Any fees you have to pay for your 'pitch' (another 'overhead').

□ The cost of fliers advertising your whelks (marketing costs – yet another 'overhead').

□ The number of tubs of whelks you sell (sales units).

□ The price per tub you sell them for (sales price).

So our much-derided whelk stall has become a little less simple as a business to measure and manage, but the essentials are still simple: to manage the stall to achieve maximum sustained net profit per week.

The purpose of Fred's whelk stall budget is simply to put figures on all the above essentials and to relate them all to his objective (i.e. net profit per week in this case), thus giving Fred the essential tool to manage and judge the success of his business. Anything else is, for our purposes, a superfluous complication.

So, just to finish our example, Fred's weekly whelk stall budget might look like this:

Sales
Sales units: 500 tubs of six cooked and seasoned whelks
Sales price: £1.75 per tub
Total sales turnover: *£875* (£1.75 × 500)

Direct costs
Wholesale costs of 3,000 whelks: £300
Condiments, gas, packaging and
other daily raw materials: £30
Total: *£330*

Gross Profit
£875 – £330 =   £545 (i.e. 62% of sales turnover)

Overheads
Pitch rental per week in the market: £100
Advertising fliers: £15
Bank interest on the loan for the
stall and equipment: £10

Wages for part-time assistant: £150
Total: *£275*

Net profit
£545 – £275 =   £270 per week

Making business decisions

Now you can see what a useful tool a budget is. Without it, our whelk stallholder could not answer the sorts of question that arise every day in a trading business. For example:

☐   The market landlord is increasing our pitch cost from £100 to £120. We can't increase our prices as we are already more than our competitors. How many more tubs would we have to sell to make the same profit as before?

☐   We tried selling at £1.95 per tub for a week and sales dropped to 475 tubs – is this better or worse for us?

☐   I could sell 400 tubs a week without my part-time assistant. Is he worth employing?

☐   A local restaurant says they would buy 50 tubs a week of our cooked whelks but would only pay £1.10 each. We can get the extra wholesale stock at the same cost price. Is this worth saying 'yes' to?

You can see that such everyday business questions, where decisions are usually required quickly, are impossible to answer without an 'economic sketch' of your business – i.e. a budget. It really is that important.

Put lots of careful thought into your annual budget, use sensible assumptions and compare regularly actual results against the budget. Your budget will be the financial basis for your management of the business, and poor budgeting often leads to business failure. You don't need to be a mathematician or accountant, but you do need to apply a disciplined and commonsense approach.

Returning a moment to the politicians trading jibes, one might reflect how much the taxpayer may have saved if Fred had been allowed to do the budget for the Millennium Dome. He could have demonstrated on the back of an envelope that a £400 million building could not possibly be an economic success in a 12-month trading life, even if it was the most popular day out in the UK and charged a price most families would baulk at. Fred would never have made such a foolish business decision.

As it happens, the Dome *was* the most popular tourist attraction that year, but was an unmitigated economic disaster. Lesson: whelk stall, Dome or B&B, budgeting is absolutely essential!

Why budgeting is vital

We hope all this will demonstrate two things:

1. A good budget is a sketch of the economic essentials of your business and how these relate to your financial objectives.

2. It must be accurate within reason and based on sound assumptions, but need not (and should not) be overcomplicated. And no jargon is necessary!

Combining the budgetary essentials above with a spreadsheet tool such as Microsoft Excel gives you a fast, easy and flexible way of constructing, adjusting and monitoring your business against your budget.

CASE STUDY: EXAMPLE BUDGET

Budgets can be as sophisticated and complex as you like, but we are keeping to the essentials here. Your budget should contain all your key financial assumptions, related to each other in the format of a simple 'profit and loss account'. It might look like the one opposite.

Annual budget for Rose Cottage B&B

Assumptions

Room price per night (average for year):	£65
Number of rooms:	three
Occupancy rate (average for year):	55%
Direct costs* (average per room per night):	£9
Proportion of house used by paying guests**:	36%

Notes

* The total costs you incur per night per room (e.g. breakfast ingredients, laundry, toiletries, newspapers, cleaning materials, etc.).

** By floor area (i.e. floor area of guest areas, divided by total floor area of the building).

Using the above assumptions, your annual budget may look something like this:

Forecast revenue (income, or 'sales turnover')

£65 × 3 rooms × 365 days × 55% =	£39,146

Less direct costs:

365 × 3 × 55% = 602 room-nights @ £9 =	£5,420

Gross profit: **£33,726**
(86% of turnover)

Expenditure (i.e. 'overheads'):

Gas, electricity, water, insurance and council tax:	
£4,250 × 36% =	£1,530
Telephone for B&B business use:	£225
Printing, stationery and postage:	£100
Advertising and marketing:	£1,300
Subscription to local tourism website:	£40
Total expenditure:	£3,195

Forecast net profit: **£30,531**

25

Clearly, this is the most simplified example. You may want to split some of the key headings. For example, you might break down your 'advertising and marketing' budget into online keyword advertising, magazines, official tourist websites, etc.

The principles are clear, however: once your budget is mapped out, you can see what changing one or more variables does to your 'bottom line' – for instance, reducing your assumed occupancy to 50% or increasing it to 60%. If your budget is on a spreadsheet program such as Microsoft Excel, this is quick and easy.

The budgeting exercise also forces you to calculate important figures like your direct costs per room per night – and your detailed workings on this will also form part of your budget.

Note that we have left out the lines below 'net profit' – taxation and net profit after tax. They are vital to you, though! We only omit them as they will depend entirely on your own tax circumstances. Get professional advice and build an estimate of your tax liability into your budget.

5
MEASURING SUCCESS

Measuring success is vital in any business. In putting together your business plan, you will have set your overall financial objectives. Your budget would have quantified these in terms of a few key success measurements. Now you need to see how well (or badly) you are actually doing in relation to these.

If you are doing better (ahead of your business plan), besides congratulating yourself, you have accrued some extra financial credit, to invest in the business, to take out of the business (if you have already allowed for and covered necessary reinvestment) or to act as a financial 'cushion' against unexpected costs or lean periods.

If you are doing less well than your original business plan, don't panic but *do* realise that your planned returns will not be there. So you need to adjust as you go along to get back to where you hoped to be. The first thing to do is calmly and dispassionately to look at the facts and figures of your actual current trading and compare these with those used in your business plan. How far out are they? Which ones are out and which are OK?

For instance, you may have budgeted for 65% occupancy and achieved 67% – well done! But you may have only achieved an average room rate of £44, after all the discounts you gave to get the bookings coming in, instead of the £55 you budgeted for.

Look at a balanced set of measurements

Success is a combination of many things: a good occupancy rate, a good average room rate, low marketing cost per booking, low direct costs per booking (e.g. breakfast and linen costs), well controlled overheads and low cancellation and complaint/refund rates. Only if all (or at least most) of these are happening will success follow.

It is no good focusing on any one success factor – occupancy, for example – at the expense of all others because you can have 100% occupancy and fail financially if your achieved room rates are much too low, and your marketing costs and overheads are much too high.

The message is: always look at a *balanced* set of measurements of your success. In the business world, these are called 'KPIs' (key performance indicators), but that is simply a jargon label.

KPIs

Fred has never heard of KPIs but he knows that his whelk stall will be successful if his *gross profit percentage* (GP%) is 60%+ and if his *unit sales* are at least 480 tubs per week. He always knows on a daily basis what he is buying and selling his whelks for, and how many tubs sell each day, so he has an immediate and accurate grasp of his two KPIs that the Finance Director of a FTSE 100 plc company, fighting their way through oceans of data compiled by others, would kill for.

You would not always know it from business textbooks or seminars, but business is not about the jargon, it's about the fundamentals. Fred is in a better position to manage his business than the plc Finance Director because he grasps the fundamentals and is closer to them and manages them directly every day. So can you with your B&B.

In our case, the KPIs we should focus on include:

☐ occupancy rate (average % of rooms filled); and

☐ average achieved price per room sold (ARR or average room rate).

These are the two key measurements in the hotel sector. Other commonly used measurements effectively combine the two. For example:

- ☐ RevPAR – (average) revenue per available room; or

- ☐ total sales per week or month.

RevPAR

This is much discussed in the hotel industry. The report below, for example, appeared on *e-TID* (the electronic *Travel Industry Digest*) on 5 August 2010:

Coalition cuts could check recovery

London hotels are in a 'league of their own' as their recovery outpaces the regions, according to PricewaterhouseCoopers. But the business consultancy warns that the government's austerity plans and public sector cuts will dampen the revival in the capital and regions.

An update to the PwC LLP Hotel Forecast shows – despite the ash cloud, strikes and bad weather – the average London RevPAR (revenue per available room) climbed from £87 in H1 2009 to £95 a year later.

In the first six months of 2010, London hotels' occupancy levels broke records for Q1 and Q2 in previous years. As a result of higher occupancy, these hotels have reduced discounting and are seeing more profitability at last, said PwC.

Hotels in the provinces, which are more dependent on domestic business travel, saw H1 RevPAR rise 1.2% to almost £39, while London hotels witnessed an increase of 9.2%.

Apart from tourist centres, such as York and Edinburgh, the north and south performance remain divided.

Business visits to the UK increased by 2% in the first half of 2010, compared to the 26% decline seen in Q109. Leisure visits in the same period slipped by 4%.

Branded budget operators are starting to see better times, as are luxury, said the report.

Several international operators reported seeing a return of the high-end business traveller to upscale hotels.

Overall for the half-year London luxury ARR (Average Room Rate) has seen a 7% gain to £235.

Liz Hall, head of hotels research at PwC, said: 'London is still driving the UK recovery, underpinned by solid ARR gains of over 6%, as the business mix reflects more transient midweek travellers.

'However, consumer confidence may take a tumble this winter as government cuts, VAT increase from 15% last year to 20% from January 2011, and a failure of incomes to keep pace with inflation starts to hit disposable income.'

If public sector budgets are slashed by 25%, PwC estimates this could have the effect of reducing its current forecast for 2010 RevPAR by 0.4% to 2.7% and for 2011 by 0.8% to 3.9%.

As an example to explain RevPAR, if you have three rooms, and charge £60 per room per night, your theoretical maximum revenue per week is £60 × 3 × 7 nights = £1,260. In reality, of course, you will not have all your rooms sold at the full price every night (if you do, *we'd* like to read *your* book!). Looking at this week (7 nights): if, say, one room is sold for four nights, one for three and one for two nights, that is nine 'room-nights' (another term you will need to use a lot in this business). If they were sold at full price apart from one night sold at your single-occupancy rate of £45, then your revenue this week was:

8 nights at £60:	£480
1 night at £45:	£45
Total:	£525

Now, with three rooms, the total number of 'available rooms' this week was 3 × 7 nights = 21. So your RevPAR this week was £525/21 = £25, meaning that your average 'take' per available room per night is £25.

The relationship between the RevPAR figure for any given period and your room rate is a good measure of success. In the above example, our actual £25 RevPAR is under half (to be precise, 42%) of our £60 room rate.

Maximising RevPAR can clearly be achieved by:

□ increasing your occupancy rate (selling more room-nights);

□ increasing your price (or decreasing any discounts you give);

□ selling more rooms as double rather than single occupancy;

□ selling more rooms with extra beds for family occupancy;

□ (if you have differential room pricing) selling a higher proportion of your higher-priced rooms.

RevPAR is useful in the hotel industry as it can be used as a comparator between different hotels within a group, or between hotel groups, etc. In your case as the owner of a B&B there will probably be no opportunity to compare RevPAR figures with others, nor would it be of much interest to you in all probability unless it related to your nearest competitors. So another way of measuring the same combination of occupancy and actual achieved price may be preferable to you: simply, the *total sales* of your B&B (excluding meals and beverages) measured over a unit of time – a week, a month, a quarter, a season or even a weekend.

Total sales in any time period actually gives you the same information as RevPAR but expressed overall rather than on a 'per room' basis. Assuming that you have not added or closed any rooms, comparing total sales between two similar periods will be the same as comparing RevPAR between the two periods.

We mention this because we feel that most B&B owners will feel no need to calculate RevPAR but will be happy simply comparing their total B&B sales figure between periods. After all, it equates to your total gross revenue (if you don't sell meals or drinks, it will be the same as your total gross revenue), so it is a very important figure which should always be at the top of your mind!

The measurements above, of course, measure the income side of the business only. Although in a B&B we do not have a 'raw material' to buy in as Fred does with his whelks, we too need to keep a close eye on the outgoings. In a B&B, these are mainly overheads (i.e. advertising and marketing, insurance, cleaning, etc.). The closest we come to a raw material cost is the cost of our property (mortgage, maintenance, utilities, etc.), which can be expressed as a cost per day per guest bedroom, but in our case this is an overhead – it is a fixed cost, however many bookings we make.

Direct costs and gross profit (GP)

There *are* some direct costs per booking: breakfast ingredients, cleaning, room consumables (soap, lavatory paper, shampoo, bin bags, tea and coffee, etc.) and laundry costs. These also can be calculated pretty accurately on a per-room, per-night basis. But the important thing to recognise about the B&B business model is that these 'direct' costs are very small relative to the gross sales income. A typical figure might be £3 per night direct costs against a sale of £60 per night, in which case 95% of the room price is 'gross profit' (GP).

In this example, £3 per room-night is your 'variable' or 'direct' cost, so any revenue above that level is a 'contribution' to your bottom line (i.e. to overheads and ultimately to profits). So selling a room at the last minute at half price (£30) gives you a £27 (£30 – £3) contribution, not a £30 loss. The concept of contribution is one to keep in mind in planning all your marketing activities.

Note: these calculations ignore any valuation of your own time (assuming that you will be doing the work yourselves). This is valid if you would otherwise be unemployed, but if you have other sources of income you can turn to, you must bear these alternatives in mind because there is no point in accepting a contribution from a discounted B&B booking which makes you less money than you could have made from an alternative revenue source in the working time necessary. In practice, you should have in mind a *minimum contribution* you will accept for a booking: in effect your minimum wage for the work involved.

The fact that the gross profit percentage (GP%) is so high – and thus contribution starts at such a low level of sales – in an accommodation business like a B&B is very important and has big implications for how the business should be managed – particularly as far as marketing and pricing are concerned. We consider these later.

6
PRICING

What do we mean by 'pricing' and why is it important? Many people new to business (and some veterans who should know better!) underestimate the importance of pricing and so don't give it much thought or priority. The assumption is often, look at what your competitors are charging and copy them, or slightly undercut them.

Devising your pricing structure is one of the most important things you will do and will have a huge influence on your success.

Pricing, of course, can't be done in a vacuum and you do have to be aware of the marketplace you are in. However, you also have to consider the 'product' you are offering compared with that of your competitors, and your own costs come into the equation too.

Think through your pricing

To start at the beginning, 'pricing' is the discipline of setting your charges to your customers for your services – both the *levels* of these charges and the *pricing structure and conditions*. So in B&B terms, pricing does *not* mean simply coming up with one figure, your room rate per night. It means thinking through the market size, consumer demands, competitive capacity and pressure, and your own cost structure, then setting a framework whereby you can achieve the highest overall profitability.

This framework may typically include:

☐ seasonal pricing;

☐ differential weekend/midweek pricing;

☐ special prices for key dates (bank holidays, half term, local festivals, etc.);

☐ differential pricing for single occupancy and multiple (e.g. family) occupancy;

☐ duration supplements or discounts (e.g. a supplement for single night stays at weekends or discounts for longer stays); and

☐ restrictions (e.g. no one-night bookings at weekends, three night minimums in half term, etc.).

Pricing is one of the key elements of marketing and has a critical effect on the success of a business. Yet it is neglected by many because it is seen as dull, difficult and figure based and so much less glamorous than playing with new logos or advertising campaigns.

Our advice is: persevere and spend a good bit of thinking time on your pricing – not just at first but as you go along, when you should be regularly testing different promotional pricing and tweaking your price framework according to experience.

Balancing the intelligent and the simple

Try to make your pricing:

☐ **intelligent**: designed with consumer demand and your business needs in mind; and

☐ **simple**: easy to communicate to the customer and easily understood by the customer.

Clearly, it is a question of balance between the intelligence of your pricing, which may lead to complexity, and the simplicity. It is always worth considering a relatively simple basic price structure (two or three seasons at most, and weekend supplements are understood and expected), with a series of temporary 'special offers' applied.

As we noted in Chapter 5, the fact that the gross profit percentage (GP%) is so high in an accommodation business like a B&B is very important, especially in pricing. Another vital and unique thing is the 'perishability' of our stock. David's grandmother, who ran a 57-bedroom hotel on Brighton seafront for over 40 years, always used to say 'an empty room is a dead loss'. If you don't sell tonight's rooms tonight, you can't ever sell tonight again.

Price according to demand

A third factor to mention with accommodation marketing is that, unlike stock available in a store, there is almost no 'substitution effect' between different dates or periods. In other words, in a store, if you discount your stock during your annual sale, you will hit sales at other times because people may have bought more when the price was lower, and some people may hold off buying if they think a sale is imminent. In a B&B, however, if you reduce your room rate from Sunday to Thursday, this will *not* mean that those who would have booked for Friday and Saturday will book midweek instead.

So price according to demand. If Friday and Saturday are generally full, charge more for those nights. And if midweek is generally empty, try promotional pricing (e.g. '£10 off your second night', 'third night half price' or '£25 off your fourth night') to promote occupancy. If need be, reduce your standard midweek rate.

Don't forget, if your price was £60 and you were not getting bookings, and you then discounted or reduced it to £50 and got bookings, you have not 'lost' £10 but 'gained' £50 for each booking. Your overheads must be paid whether you are full or empty.

Of course, intelligent pricing requires you to understand the demand pattern in your local market. This will only come with time and experience, so at first you will have to use your instinct, and then carefully monitor demand and adapt your pricing accordingly.

Pricing framework variables

SEASONAL PRICING

This is very basic, almost universal in the tourism industry, and easy for customers to understand. Most hotels and B&Bs have an out-of-season, shoulder season and high-season rate, and some may have different rates for almost every month of the year. Always remember the 'keep it simple' part of our equation, though. Don't forget that you, your partner and anyone else who handles booking inquiries needs to have the pricing confidently on the tip of the tongue. Any confusion or a proliferation of different rates to quote to each inquirer will not encourage people to book with you.

As with all our pricing tips, you need to start with the actual seasonality of your own marketplace – i.e. your location and type of accommodation. If you are a city-centre B&B and get a lot of business customers, your seasonality will probably be much flatter and year-round than for a tourist B&B in a seaside resort. The seaside B&B may well have extreme seasonality, being very busy for Easter, May half-term and the summer holidays but virtually dead the rest of the year. If this describes your business, then you must charge the maximum you can in your high season consistent with virtually full occupancy (you cannot afford empty rooms in this period) and take your prices as low as they need to go out of season to achieve viable occupancy. You will probably find it not worth staying open at all in very low season (November to February, for instance).

DIFFERENTIAL WEEKEND/MIDWEEK PRICING

How important this is to you will again depend on your location and clientele. If leisure short breaks are your mainstay (as they would typically be for a country B&B, for instance), then you will probably find no difficulty filling Friday and Saturday nights but will struggle to get bookings for Sunday to Thursday. Here, you should end up with a sharp price differential.

B&Bs in town or city locations, on the other hand, may attract some non-leisure clientele – i.e. businesspeople staying for work reasons. The business market is very different from the leisure market, most obviously in being a midweek market. If you get business bookings, these will typically be midweek, for one night, in single occupancy. If you run a townhouse B&B in a business district, business bookings may be your mainstay and, in this case, you will have to price down weekends to try to encourage some weekend occupancy.

SPECIAL PRICES FOR KEY DATES

In the leisure market, bank holidays will be popular. There may also be some local events that are popular – for instance, the International Festival in Edinburgh, the Chelsea Flower Show in London and many other smaller festivals, shows and events which result in increased localised demand. We have an example in Sherborne, the Dorset town where our own B&B is based. Here in the third week of August for a few years, the 'IronMan UK' triathlon has taken place, bringing 1,500 athletes and their families, friends and spectators to a town with only three hotels and a handful of B&Bs. Consequently, a higher price could be obtained for the four or five days of the event than the rest of the year.

You may not want to raise your price above your highest season rate for an event in high season, but you would lose potential revenue if you priced a special date during low season at the low season rate. In such a case, you may want to say, for instance 'high season is July, August, Easter, May half-term and the dates of the town festival'.

Christmas and New Year is a very specific market, based around meals and entertainment. Most B&Bs close for this period for a rest but if you serve meals and drinks and have open fires in winter, you may find that this is a key profit-making time for you.

DIFFERENTIAL PRICING FOR OCCUPANCY

In practice, in hotels or B&Bs there is never just a 'room rate'. Single, double and multiple (e.g. family) occupancy are all usually priced differently.

Of course, the 'standard' occupancy of a room is two, as people tend to come in twos, like the animals in Noah's Ark. This means that most, if not all, your rooms should be for two.

It is *never* worth making a room a true 'single' room – i.e. with one single bed – unless it is too small to fit a double bed. Even your single travellers (especially business people) will prefer (and probably expect) to sleep in a double bed. In practice, if you have no single rooms, you should accommodate your single bookers in a room for two: a double or twin.

If your costs are on a per-room basis, why should single travellers expect to pay less than couples? In rational terms, a single booker uses the same room facilities and eats one breakfast rather than two, so should expect to pay the price of a room for two, less the price of one breakfast. It is as simple and unarguable as that.

However, the hotel and holiday industry in the UK has historically charged on a per-person basis (mainly because it makes the prices look cheaper), so the single occupancy differential has to be presented as a 'single-occupancy supplement' to the (half double) per-person price rather than a discount against the double-room price. This in presentational terms *looks* as if it discriminates against single people (even though it does not), and journalists have encouraged consumers to feel cheated by writing many a piece on the dreaded single-occupancy supplement.

THE 'SINGLE SUPPLEMENT' MYTH

'In the travel world, there are perhaps no two words more guaranteed to elicit an incendiary response among solo holidaymakers as these: "single supplement". Internet forums simmer with remarks about the injustice of having to pay extra for seemingly using less' – so began an article in the *Daily Mail* (6 September 2009). We have lost count of the number of articles, 'readers' rants', blogs and Internet posts about the so-called 'iniquities' of the single supplement, and the evils of the B&Bs and hotels guilty of this 'outrage'.

It is time to shoot this down – as it is a myth and a nonsense, as a moment's common sense will show. We need not be at all apologetic about this issue – it simply needs explaining properly to our guests.

Take a B&B charging a fairly typical £70 for a double room or £50 for single occupancy.

It is only because of the British habit – led by tour operators – to quote on a per-person basis that this is seen as couples paying £35 per person, and singles being 'penalised' by being charged an 'extra' £15 – 'paying extra for seemingly using less', as the *Daily Mail* puts it. So unfair!

But hold on a second – what is the B&B offering? Bed and breakfast, of course: 1) a room; and 2) breakfast. If we say breakfast in our example accounts for, say, £8, our couple are paying £16 for breakfast and £54 for the room (£70 – £16). That is the 'standard' price, as of course most bookings are for two sharing the room.

Our single traveller, paying £50, is thus paying £8 breakfast and £42 (£50 – £8) for the room in single occupancy. The same room that couples pay £54 for. So in reality, the B&B has given the single traveller a discount, in this case of over 22% (£12 on £54). And yet the single booker, encouraged by the ranters, may well feel resentful at paying an 'extra' £15! If they were truly paying the same for bed and breakfast, the single booker in our example should pay £62 (£70 – £8), the double price less one breakfast. Anything less is a room discount.

ALARM BELL

Don't be apologetic. Try not to encourage the single-occupancy supplement myth by only quoting 'per person'. Try to help guests understand that a 'supplement' is often in reality a discount!

The fact is, though, that there is a general market expectation that a single occupancy rate should be discounted by much more than the price of one breakfast as compared with the double occupancy rate. As this is the market expectation and your competitors are likely to be following suit, you will probably not be able to avoid giving single people what amounts in fact to a room discount.

This is an instance where you *can* be hit with a substitution effect: if someone books a double or twin room for single occupancy, you lose money compared with booking that room as a double. It follows that you will always rather sell every room in double rather than single occupancy.

Set your single-occupancy price as near to the 'double less one breakfast' level as you can, though if this leads to a net loss of bookings (i.e. you do not gain double bookings to make up for the loss in singles), then this may need adjusting because, as we can't repeat often enough, an empty room is a dead loss.

Just as a single-occupancy booking is a negative factor against the double or twin 'standard', you can gain positively by selling higher occupancy – e.g. adding extra beds to make a triple or family room. Here we must be consistent with our stance on single occupancy: based on fundamental economics, if the third person occupies an extra bed in a double or twin room, you cannot charge the same per person for the third person, as this would in effect be a 50% supplement for the same room. The third person is having a breakfast and an extra change of linen and towels, so the supplement should reflect this. At the time of writing, we charge £35 per person in a double (i.e. £70 for the room) and £15 for a third person in an extra bed.

DURATION SUPPLEMENTS OR DISCOUNTS

If you have never run a hotel or B&B before, we can tell you that one of the biggest things you learn almost from day one is the importance of longer duration bookings. Getting one two-night booking is vastly better than getting two successive one-night bookings, even though your income, RevPAR and occupancy figures are the same.

Why? If you compare two one-night bookings with one two-night booking:

☐ you have two room changeovers rather than one: double the work;

☐ you have two arrivals rather than one: twice the waiting;

☐ you have twice the laundry bill, assuming you don't wash linen on day two; and

☐ your bill on things like soaps will double.

So one of your top priorities will always be to encourage longer stays. You can do this, for example, with a supplement for single-night stays at weekends or various discounts for longer stays – third night half-price, fourth night free, etc.

Believe us, one of the holy grails in this business is getting a good number of longer bookings. At our own B&B, we gain from a good, steady year-round seasonality in Sherborne, but outside the spring and summer season much of the demand is for one and two-night bookings, so we suffer from a relatively high average workload per room-night. We are always delighted to get four-, five- or six-night bookings and do our best to encourage them.

The incentive you offer for a longer-duration booking need not, of course, be 'money off': it is better to give an 'added value' incentive, something which has a higher perceived value to the customer than it actually costs you financially.

An ideal incentive is a free bottle of wine or champagne, but (and not many B&B owners realise this) it is illegal for B&Bs to give alcoholic drinks away free, unless you have a licence. If you have a licence, try an offer such as 'a complimentary half-bottle of champagne with every booking of four nights or more between the dates of X and Y'.

RESTRICTIONS

The incentives we discussed earlier will encourage longer bookings, bookings at weak times, etc. Sometimes, though, you will want to go further and disallow certain types of bookings at certain times. This is what we mean by 'restrictions'.

For instance, you may get a lot of family demand at half term, and these are attractive bookings for you: family occupancy and longer durations. If you have, say, four rooms, accepting even a couple of one-night bookings during half-term might well mean that you have to turn away 50% of the longer family bookings you would have obtained. As a B&B owner, few things are more painful and frustrating than turning down a five-night booking for a family because you have a one-night booking in single occupancy in the middle of the period required!

The answer in these situations is to make a restriction: for example in the case above, 'a three-night minimum applies during half term' (or four nights – it is your judgement).

The most common instance of a restriction is against one-night bookings on Fridays or Saturdays. This has great logic to it, but taking the plunge and putting that rule in place is difficult, especially if a good proportion of your weekend bookings have been one-nighters up to now. There is no easy answer: such decisions are part of life for the business owner. It's what makes running a business so challenging – and so rewarding when you get it right.

7
CLASSIFYING YOUR B&B
FOR BUSINESS PURPOSES

Applying for planning permission

IS YOUR PROPERTY A HOME OR A BUSINESS?

The definition of a B&B is not a clear-cut one as far as officialdom is concerned, and indeed different departments apply different criteria. You might assume that, logically, a decision is taken by a government department against well established criteria as to whether your premises will be classed as a business or a home, and that this would determine what you can do to the premises (planning) as well as how the premises are taxed (council tax or business rates).

That would indeed be logical and 'joined up'. Of course, it doesn't happen. The first thing to note is that the planning definition of a B&B as opposed to a home, although very broadly similar in principle to the local tax definition, is determined entirely separately and against different criteria and by different people at different times. It is possible, if perhaps unlikely, to have a premises classed as a home for tax purposes (thus paying council tax), but classed as a business for planning purposes – or indeed vice versa.

Fire, hygiene and other legislation is all different again and administered separately by different departments. The whole thing is a minefield, and expecting any connection between all these different branches of government is the first thing you must give up.

PLANNING – C3 OR C1?

One fundamental area is planning. Planning legislation defines the 'use classes' of property and thus what you are allowed to do with the property.

A B&B which is a family home within which paying guests stay occasionally is primarily, according to any reasonable person's way of thinking, a home. Broadly, the planning regulations reflect this, but (as with all government regulation) it is by no means as simple as that!

The first thing to note is that there are only two planning-use classes into which a B&B can fall: it can be either C3, a 'Dwelling House' – i.e. a home – or C1, a 'Hotel'. The C1 class:

> *includes not only hotels, but also motels, bed and breakfast premises, boarding and guest houses. These are premises which provide a room as temporary accommodation on a commercial, fee-paying basis, where meals can be provided but where residential care is not provided (ODPM (now Department for Communities and Local Government) Circular 03/2005:* Changes of Use of Buildings and Land *).*

Under planning-use classes, a 500-bedroom hotel is in the same planning category as a B&B.

So the critical question becomes: what makes the difference between planning-use class C3 and C1? When does the planning authority class your house as equivalent to the Heathrow Hilton, as opposed to a family home?

Amazingly, there is *no* guidance for local authorities from the government department responsible for planning (the Department for Communities and Local Government, or DCLG) as to when a change of use from C3 to C1 (from home to hotel) should be applied for. It is up to the discretion of each local authority. Some may be happy for busy B&Bs to be in class C3 (home), and others may try to insist that if a householder lets even one room to one paying guest, they must apply for a change of use to C1 – the planning category shared by, for example, the Heathrow Hilton.

From the point of view of the fair and consistent treatment of B&Bs, this situation is clearly very unsatisfactory. In this book we can only try to supply you with enough of the general information for you to be able to give a reasoned and informed reply to your local authority, if they are demanding that you must apply for change of use.

For a B&B in what is primarily your family home, and you do not accommodate more than six paying guests at any one time, you should not normally have to apply for a 'change of use' from C3 to C1. The key is in the 'primary use' of the premises – and here local authorities apply very different approaches in different areas. Some say that if 50% or more of the building is used by guests – perhaps including the lounge and dining room and corridors, say, measured by surface area (the actual 50% test is not laid down in law, and each local authority may look at it differently) – then a change of use should be sought.

Ensure that guests are aware of the check-out time for leaving their room so that you are not faced with the situation of having no changeover time between guests. This can be helped by offering those who are leaving the chance to store their luggage in a public area downstairs so that you have access to clean their room ready for the next guest. If the unexpected happens and your new guests turn up early they can also store their luggage or wait in a public room until their rooms are ready, offering them a tray of tea or coffee while they are waiting.

In some cases we know about, people who have been running a B&B in their home for decades have suddenly been told by their local authority that they must apply for a change of use, even though there has been no change to the activities which the local authority has been accepting in a primarily residential building. This understandably causes extreme consternation – if the owner accepts that they need to apply for a change of use then is not granted it, they would be in the position of having their livelihood or part of it summarily taken away. And the fact that the local authority is suddenly telling them that they *must* apply for a change of use seems to imply that, at the very least, that authority feels there are grounds for their planning-use class to be changed.

This is happening despite their being no negative impact on neighbouring properties or the character of the area from the (secondary) B&B use and despite there being a significant economic benefit for the area through tourism from the B&B use of premises – something which government guidance asks local authorities to take into account in their planning decisions. This area of planning regulation and enforcement is messy, inconsistent and illogical and it results in the highly unfair and unjust treatment of homeowners who choose to attract tourism business to their area by offering B&B accommodation in their homes.

In planning law:

> the Courts have held that the first thing to consider in determining whether a material change of use has occurred (or will occur) is the existing primary use of the land [or premises]. Each case will always be a matter for individual determination by fact and degree. In particular, local planning authorities will need to take into consideration more than just the amount of floor space occupied by the different uses. For example, in the case of a premises which incorporates restaurant as well as pub or bar use, the local planning authority will need to determine whether the existing primary use of the premises is as a restaurant (A3), or as a drinking establishment (A4), or a mixed use. This will depend on such matters as whether customers come primarily to eat, drink, or both. It is the main purpose of that use that is to be considered. (ODPM Circular 03/2005: Changes of Use of Buildings and Land).

So we are afraid that there are no simple, hard-and-fast rules we can spell out for you. Whether you will be in danger of your local authority telling you that you must apply for a change of use is something of a lottery, depending on where you live as well as the circumstances of your B&B.

Do remember that it is the 'primary use' and 'main purpose' that apply in determining the planning-use class – C3 or C1. If your premises are your home, especially if you have no other home, that is a very good indication that the primary use of the premises is as a home. Other arguments which are persuasive are that:

☐ most of the area of the building is home rather than B&B;

☐ income from the B&B is not your sole income;

☐ your B&B activity is small scale (especially if the maximum is six B&B guests – see below); and

☐ your B&B activity would not be justified as a standalone commercial business – in other words, that it has to be subsidiary to (and indeed subsidised by) the main purpose of the premises, as your family home.

Also remember that planning regulations are all about *impacts* on neighbouring properties and the locality and its resources and amenities. So for planning purposes, your turnover or profits are completely irrelevant; what is relevant is the effect your business has on those around you – e.g. parking, the comings and goings of guests, noise, excessive use of services (such as refuse collection) – compared with a typical home, and the visual impact of signs or other features of the B&B. This is important to bear in mind when dealing with your planning department. If your business has no negative impact on your neighbours, then what planning grounds can the local authority have for requiring a change of use to C1?

Determining which tax you will have to pay

There is a critical difference to you as the owner between your property being treated as a home as opposed to it being treated as business premises. A home will be subject to council tax, will be allowed to use normal domestic services (e.g. refuse collection) and will generally be subject to less monitoring and regulation than business premises, which will pay business rates instead of council tax.

The taxation of your property is determined by different criteria from those used by planning. Here it is not local impacts but the scale of a property's use as a business that is relevant.

Again, there is a primary-use test, but the difference is that the department concerned, the Valuation Office Agency (VOA), has published some reasonably clear criteria for differentiating between a B&B subject to council tax and one subject to business rates. The following basic guide to the rating of guest houses and B&B accommodation comes from the VOA:

What is a rateable value?

Every non-domestic property has a rateable value, apart from those properties that are exempt from rates. The rateable value broadly represents the annual rent the property could have been let for on the open market on a particular date, on full repairing and insuring terms. For the current rating list, this date was set as 1 April 2003.

What factors may be taken into account in arriving at the rateable value?

In arriving at the rateable value, the actual rents which operators pay may be taken into account. In addition other factors may also be taken into account such as:

- *The number of bedrooms, whether singles, doubles or family rooms, basic or ensuite*

- *Location and quality of the accommodation*

- *The presence of non-resident restaurant facilities*

When is a Bed and Breakfast property domestic?

The property will be domestic and therefore subject to council tax rather than business rates if:

- *You intend not to provide short stay accommodation for more than six persons at any one time within the coming year; and*

- *The property is your sole or main residence and the bed and breakfast use is subsidiary to the private use*

What factors are considered when applying the 'subsidiary use test'?

The 'subsidiary use test' is to ensure, as far as possible, that whilst the provision of limited short stay accommodation in a person's own home will not be subject to rating, this exemption will not extend to those where bed and breakfast is a significant business enterprise.

1. Accommodation used

This is the amount of a property used for B&B at any one time; if half or more of the whole house is used for guests at any time that property is likely to be rated.

2. Adaptation to a property

If adaptations carried out specifically to benefit guests alter the character of the property beyond that of a private house, then the B&B use may not be subsidiary and the property is likely to be rated.

Example: *The installation of additional wash basins, bathrooms or ensuite facilities, fire precautions such as fire doors, alarms and extinguishers.*

[We would comment here that where building regulations require fire doors, alarms and extinguishers even in a private dwelling (for example to provide a 'protected means of escape' within a building of two or more storeys), it would be difficult to use their presence as an argument that the premises are not primarily a dwelling.]

3. Nature of use

Factors such as whether the property is open all year round, serves evening meals or has a licence are taken into account when deciding if it is a subsidiary use.

Is my rateable value the same as the rates I will pay?

No. Rateable values are a key factor in the calculation of business rates but they are not the rates bill. Local authorities are responsible for calculating actual rates bills and for collecting rates and will use the rateable value in working out how much you have to pay. The local authority will apply the multiplier, (a rate in the pound), then deduct any reliefs that are applicable. In England the multiplier is set by the Department for Communities and Local Government and in Wales the multiplier is set by the Welsh Assembly Government.

The local authority will also work out any transitional adjustment. The transitional adjustment limits the amount by which your rates bill changes following a revaluation. There is no transitional relief in Wales.

From what date will the Bed & Breakfast property be rated?

Generally, a property will be entered in the rating list with effect from the date that it becomes available for use as a Bed and Breakfast. This date is known as the 'Effective Date'.

Can I appeal against the rating assessment?

Yes. You can appeal against both the rateable value and the Effective Date – this is known as making a 'proposal' to alter the rating list.

If you have had an entry in the 2010 rating list from 1 April 2010 you can make a single appeal against the original entry in this list at any time up until 31 March 2015. If it is a new entry into the rating list, or the entry has been altered since 1 April 2010, you will be served a notice by the Valuation Officer, against which you can make one appeal.

If at any time, a material change of circumstances affecting the property or its physical locality takes place, you are entitled to make a further appeal.

Proposals in response to a list alteration or a new entry in the 2010 list may be made up to 31 March 2015. The Effective Date of an alteration to the rating list in response to a ratepayer's appeal may be subject to certain limitations. For more information contact your local Valuation Office.

You can obtain a proposal form from your local Valuation Office or you can make an appeal online from the VOA's web site at: www.voa.gov.uk

Homes are liable to council tax and businesses for business rates. The regulations:

are intended to ensure that [B&Bs] ... will continue to be domestic property (and therefore not rateable) if: (a) it is intended that within the coming year the short stay accommodation will not be provided for more than six persons simultaneously; and (b) the proprietor intends to have his or her sole or main residence within the [property] and the short stay use will be subsidiary to the use of the [property] as the proprietor's sole or main residence.

The regulations also say:

each case will need to be judged on its merits. The emphasis must be placed on the use of the premises, whereas mere registration with the local tourist bureau would not be sufficient. It should be borne in mind that the intention of the 'subsidiary use test' is to ensure, as far as possible, that whilst the provision of limited short stay accommodation in a person's own home will not be subject to rating, this exemption will not extend to those where the main use of the property is clearly non-domestic.

For more detail, see www.voa.gov.uk

8
APPLYING FOR LICENCES

Copyright licensing

This is a highly confusing subject, and B&Bs have to face a plethora of different regulators. It seems wholly disproportionate that a very small B&B should be expected to pay three different licences to three different authorities in order to let their guests watch TV and listen to the radio and CDs or discs, for instance – and four licences if the B&B also lends DVDs or video tapes to its guests. David has suggested to policymakers within the coalition government of 2010 that the 'bonfire of the quangos' the government has proposed should include the PRS (Performing Rights Society) for Music and the Phonographic Performance Licence (PPL), which could be abolished and a new simpler, streamlined copyright licensing regime brought in including the BBC TV licence and the performers' and composers' interests represented currently by the PRS and PPL.

TV LICENCE

The first and best-known of the copyright licensing schemes is the TV licence, effectively a tax administered by the BBC that funds the BBC's output, including all its TV and radio channels (as well as, strangely perhaps, its websites and other 'free' services).

The standard TV licence that families pay covers a home but it does not cover the use of TVs by paying guests. Once you start your B&B, you should apply for a 'hotel and mobile units television licence' (hotel licence). Despite its name, the hotel licence covers accommodation, including guesthouses and B&Bs (and even campsites), as well as hotels.

The TV Licensing Authority says that you should always take out a hotel licence if you are providing televisions for the use of paying guests. While staying on your property, guests are *not* covered by their home licence. There is one exception: long-term hotel residents (i.e. those staying over 28 days) are not covered by a hotel licence. They must have an ordinary television licence.

The TV Licensing website states:

> *Hotels, hostels, campsites and mobile units must be covered by a valid TV Licence if staff or customers watch or record television programmes as they're being shown on TV. This includes the use of devices such as a TV, computer, mobile phone, games console, digital box or DVD/VHS recorder.*

A single TV licence costing (in August 2010) £145.50 will cover up to 15 accommodation units on a single site.

For further infomation, go to www.tvlicensing.co.uk

PRS FOR MUSIC

In November 2009, the British Hospitality Association (BHA) and PRS for Music (previously the Performing Rights Society) reached an agreement over music played in hotel bedrooms, ending a long-running dispute. The BHA, the trade association for hotels, restaurants and caterers, agreed to advise their members and, indeed, all hotels, guest houses and B&Bs, to pay licence fees going forward for music played in hotel and B&B bedrooms, via TV, radio or any other device. A settlement has also been reached with respect to licence fees disputed in previous years.

The PRS for Music, the organisation representing songwriters, composers and music publishers, had been in discussion with the BHA (who were acting in this matter on behalf of all hotels, guest houses and B&Bs, as the legal issues are identical for all) for many years about whether music played in a hotel bedroom requires a licence from the copyright owners (represented by the PRS for Music). The agreement follows several months of discussions after a European Court of Justice opinion confirmed that certain uses of music in hotel bedrooms *do* require a licence from the copyright holders of that music.

Debbie Mulloy, Commercial Director for the PRS for Music's public performance team, said:

> We are delighted that we have been able to work with the BHA to reach a settlement. The provision of TVs and radios in hotel bedrooms is a clear benefit to hotels and their guests, and it's good news that our members will now receive royalties for the use of their work.

Bob Cotton, Chief Executive of the BHA, said:

> It is good news that the hospitality industry will now have certainty about licences from PRS for Music for music in hotel bedrooms. This has been a very long standing dispute, but I am pleased it has been settled at last.

For B&Bs and guest houses, as for hotels, the bad news is that this agreement brings to an end the dispute (and the previous stance adopted by many B&Bs of deferring payment while the legal dispute carried on) and acknowledges that the new legal reality (after an EU change in definition) means that the PRS for Music *are* legally entitled to require B&Bs and guest houses with TVs or radios in guest rooms to pay a licence. Licences for music in guest bedrooms start from £44 plus VAT per year, for up to 15 bedrooms (more details are on the PRS website at www.prsformusic.com). The good news is that the settlement means that those who pay from 2009 onwards will *not* now be liable to pay six years' back claims to 2003, as the PRS had been pushing for.

The authors share the concerns of the Bed and Breakfast Association that B&B and guest house owners have reported 'aggressive' and 'threatening' attitudes in the PRS call-centre staff who are calling them to demand payment. We are also concerned that the PRS are trying to double charge: the minimum charge of some £44 covers up to 15 rooms and 'corridors and foyers' but, if the B&B also has a radio or TV in its lounge or breakfast room, the PRS seems to be demanding a much higher licence fee on the basis of music being played in a 'public' room. And yet for B&Bs and guest houses (unlike, say, large hotels), there is no public access and the guests whose music use is covered by the licence 'upstairs' as it were, are the same guests listening to the same music 'downstairs'.

THE PRS FOR MUSIC COMPLAINTS PROCEDURE

If you have a complaint about your treatment by PRS for Music, write to Customer Services, PRS for Music, Elwes House, 19 Church Walk, Peterborough, Cambs PE1 2UZ. If you are not satisfied with this response, you should write to the Managing Director (at the same address) stating your reasons.

If you are not satisfied with the outcome of our complaints procedure, or if you feel your complaint has not been handled correctly, you may refer your complaint to the Ombudsman for PRS for Music, on 0330 440 1601 – or see the website: www.prsformusic-ombudsman.org

We also believe there should be a reduced 'entry level' licence for small B&Bs who currently have to pay the same as a 15-bedroom hotel. The Bed and Breakfast Association will, on behalf of its members, be monitoring the legal situation in case of future opportunities for challenge, as we are disappointed that the hospitality industry has not been able to win the legal argument about the use of TVs and radios in guest bedrooms.

PPL

While PRS licences relate to the copyright in the music itself, there is a separate licence issued by the PPL which relates to the actual *recording*, whether on a CD, tape or other format. If you play music in your B&B or guest house 'in public' from a record, tape, compact disc, video, etc., you require a PPL licence.

There are two types of PPL licence. For the use of sound recordings:

☐ as background music in breakfast rooms, bars and lounges; and

☐ as a featured attraction (e.g. at dances or discos).

Following a successful court case brought by the BHA and the British Beer and Pub Association (BBPA) against the PPL about the level of fees charged for licences, the PPL has issued a form you can use to claim a refund. This refund will be the difference between the fee paid between 2006 and 2009 and the fee set by the tribunal. However, there are a couple of caveats to this refund:

☐ A refund cannot be claimed if the total repayment for the period is less than £50.

☐ If during that period you have paid your licence late, the tribunal has allowed the PPL to charge 50% more, which reduces the amount of refund you are entitled to.

For further infomation, go to www.ppluk.com

DVD CONCIERGE LICENCE (FILMBANK)

Many B&Bs offer their guests a DVD or video film library – i.e. lending guests pre-recorded films on DVD or video to watch in the comfort of their own room. However, whether you charge or not, such lending is legally considered commercial as it takes place in the context of a commercial transaction (i.e. the payment for a room on a B&B basis).

The purchase of films on DVD or video, or even receiving them free of charge (e.g. with a newspaper or magazine), confers on you the right to watch the film yourself in your home, but *not* to play the film in a commercial context, such as to paying guests.

Filmbank, part of Warner Bros, has launched the 'DVD concierge licence' to raise funds for the copyright holders (i.e. the Hollywood film studios) by allowing hotels, B&Bs or guest houses to use their own DVD libraries for lending to guests, paying for the copyright permission by means of the licence.

The following is from the Filmbank website:

Screening films without a licence is an infringement of copyright law. It is a civil, and in some cases, criminal offence to show a film in this manner without the permission of the copyright owner (the film studios) or their representatives (the licensing bodies).

What is the DVD Concierge Licence?

The DVD Concierge Licence is an annual licence payable on a per room basis. The licence will permit properties to operate DVD film libraries for guest use, whether guests are using DVD players, lap tops, games consoles or other portable devices. Properties will be able to hold an unlimited number of DVDs from the represented studios covered by the licence.

The DVD Concierge Licence is an annual licence based on the number of guest rooms in the property, however a seasonal licence is also available for properties open for a period of 8 months or less. With the DVD Concierge licence you will be covered for the use of films from many of the major Hollywood and independent studios.

For further information on the DVD concierge licence call 020 7984 5954 or go to the Filmbank website at www.filmbank.co.uk and look for 'DVD concierge licence'.

Applying for an alcohol licence

The question of whether to offer drinks to guests is a big decision. If you offer evening meals on a regular basis, then obtaining a licence will almost certainly be worth while as many people will want drinks – especially wine – with their dinner, and this will be a viable source of additional profit to the restaurant area of your business.

For the traditional B&B serving no meals except breakfast, this is not such a clear-cut decision. The benefits are that, potentially, serving alcoholic drinks may become a profitable sideline and that being licensed may attract more clients.

Less obviously but very usefully, a licence allows you to use promotions such as the 'complimentary half-bottle of champagne with every four-night booking' we mentioned earlier in this book. It is worth repeating that, whatever you may have understood up to now, it is illegal for B&Bs to give alcoholic drinks away free, unless they are licensed. This is because caselaw has established that there is no such thing as a 'free' drink provided by a business – it always represents part of value paid for in other ways by a customer. When you think about it, this is logical because, otherwise, for instance, you could sell peanuts for £4 and give a 'free' glass of wine and never need a licence. A further advantage is that it may open up profitable sidelines, such as private functions, where much of the profit comes from the alcoholic drinks consumed.

The downsides are as follows:

- Becoming licensed is fairly expensive and involves a lot of time, paperwork and regulation.

- Serving drinks opens up a whole new area of work for you.

- You will need space for a bar and sitting area.

- You will need to invest in equipment, such as fridges, optics, glasses, ice machines, dishwashers, etc., depending on the scale of your operation and, of course, in a sufficient stock of drinks.

The Licensing Act 2003, which finally came fully into force in November 2005, changed the system completely: you now need both a 'premises licence' and a separate 'personal licence'. For the premises licence, you need to fill in a form and submit copies of plans of your premises to about seven authorities (fire, police, etc.) and publish your plans in the main local paper. For the personal licence, you need to undergo a training course typically costing between £140 and £200.

In our B&B, even though we do not serve dinner, we have chosen to go for a licence because:

- we have a bar area from when the premises were a hotel;

- we have a fairly upmarket clientele who will (we hope!) buy wine by the glass and the occasional bottle of champagne for celebrations; and

- David has always been a keen wine buff (or at least, drinker!) and plans wine-tasting events.

In many ways, the 2003 Act was a simplification and liberalisation of the previous licensing regime. It swept away the previous distinctions between serving alcohol with meals and without, for instance. In this sense it is good for B&Bs, who will also benefit from the presumption in favour of granting a licence, which is part of the Act. However, many small B&Bs may be deterred from applying for a licence because of their worries about bureaucracy, time and cost. Don't be deterred! If selling alcoholic drinks is important to you, persevere – it is not as bad as you think!

Having been part of the very first intake of new licensees (both for premises and personal licences) under the 2003 Act as it came into force on 24 November 2005, we are in an ideal position to advise you on the practicalities of how the new Act works in real life.

First, the Act separates premises licences and personal licences: your physical premises must be licensed, *and* they must be supervised by someone who also has a personal licence. The premises licence can be 'sold' with the premises (and may indeed become an asset to a new owner), whereas your personal licence stays with you and will allow you to run another licensed premises elsewhere.

PERSONAL LICENCE

This is the simplest, so we'll take it first. Basically you just fill in a form and pay the fee of £37. Of course, it is slightly more complicated than that, but not much. You need two passport photos, one signed by a town councilor, solicitor or someone similar, stating that it is a good likeness of you. You also need to run a Criminal Records Bureau (CRB) check less than a month before your personal licence application goes in to show that you don't have any disqualifying criminal convictions, and you must disclose any recent relevant convictions, including alcohol-related driving offences.

Passing an exam

The most costly and time-consuming part is that you have to pass a specified qualification for licensees. This means attending a one-day course followed by a half-day exam, costing typically between £140 and £200 (though we managed to find one for only £108.75 in 2005). The good news is that this is a one-off expense.

There are a large number of such courses, run fairly frequently in most regions, so it should not generally be a problem to book on to one at a reasonably convenient date and location – though if you have a full-time job, it will generally mean taking two consecutive days' leave. You cannot apply for your personal licence until you have taken and passed your licence holder's qualification, so check out local course dates and locations early on in your planning process.

Having not sat an exam for 22 years, it was a novel experience revising the essential points of the Licensing Act 2003, then taking the BIIAB Level 2 National Certificate for Personal Licence Holders at Yeovil College. However, it is pretty easy, and I left the examination hall after only 30 of the 40 minutes we were allowed for the paper – and I passed, although I was not told my score. The exam is multiple choice and 40 questions: you must correctly answer the first eight and must then get at least 22 of the next 32 to pass.

Renewing your licence

Your personal licence will last 10 years and is then renewable for further 10-year periods, but you only have a two-month window within which to renew, starting three months before the 10 years expires, so don't miss it or you will have to start again and take a new exam.

The only requirements thereafter which must be remembered are that you must always tell your licensing authority (i.e. the authority who granted your personal licence in the first place) of every change of address while you still hold a licence and of every 'relevant' conviction, including drink-driving convictions. Should you appear in court, you must also inform the court that you are a personal licence holder.

Besides allowing you to serve drinks at your own licensed premises, once you hold a personal licence you will be able to serve or supervise the serving of drinks in *any* licensed premises so, if you are interested in other employment (perhaps part time) in a hotel, restaurant, pub or bar, your personal licence will make you more marketable to potential employers.

PREMISES LICENCE

This is independent of the personal licence, so you can apply for it before you have sat your course and passed your personal qualification. The most involved part of this process is the application form and the premises plans you will need to submit with it. Timing is dictated by the notice periods you need to give to the public about your application, so you need to plan to submit the application on the same day as your 'public notice' advert comes out in your local paper (which typically needs booking a week in advance), and you also need to post information notices outside your premises on the same day (preferably A4, black 16-point type on pale blue paper).

The wording for these advertisements and notices is similar, and examples can be found in the public notices section of your local paper. The guidance notes in your licence application pack will also detail their contents.

Some key points to remember are as follows:

☐ **The licence will last indefinitely** (provided you pay the annual renewal fee, and do not lose the licence by abusing it!), so don't be more specific than you have to be. Don't tie yourself (and a future owner) down to specific times for ever. It is better to apply for long hours (or 24 hours) and state that 'normally' you anticipate stopping serving alcohol by midnight, for instance.

☐ **Think about the future** – including the possibility of your selling the premises – and apply for things you or a future owner *might* want to do, even if you have no current plans for them. For example, dancing, showing films or 'indoor sporting activities' (which could include billiards, darts or skittles).

☐ **Don't provoke questions or objections unnecessarily**. For example, a copy of your application goes to child protection officers, so make sure you specify that alcohol will not be served to children, that British Board of Film Classification (BBFC) guidelines will be observed in the showing of films, etc. If you leave out such details (even if they may seem obvious), your application may be delayed by a question coming back on these points.

☐ **On premises plans, mark the whole extent of your useable property for licensable activities** – again, this keeps your options open. For instance, don't only specify your currently planned bar area for the site of licensable activities. Include all areas or rooms which may conceivably be used in future. You or the next owner might want to use a current private sitting room as a dining room or function room, for instance, and if you do not include such a room now, you or your successor would have to submit a special 'licence variation' application.

We found that our licensing authority (West Dorset District Council) were very helpful. We went to see the licensing officer in Dorchester, who helped with our premises application. We would recommend that, if you can, you arrange to see your licensing officer *before* you submit your application to discuss it.

COSTING THE LICENCES

Typically, the licences break down as follows:

Personal licence application fee:	£37
Premises licence application fee:	£100 (one off)
Premises licence grant fee (annual):	£70*
Personal licensee's course fee:	£170 (one off)
Public notice ad in local paper – typically 10 cm × 1 column:	£115 (one off)
Passport photos:	£4
Photocopying – 150 pages or so at, say, 8p per page:	£12
Envelopes, postage, etc.:	£5
Total:	*£513*

* This depends on the business rateable value of your premises. If, like ours, your B&B is domestically rated rather than business rated, you will automatically fall into Band A at £70 (though this is not made clear on the application form). See Chapter 7 for when a B&B is usually rated for business rates rather than council tax.

You will also need to be in compliance with all planning, fire, health and safety and other legislation, as your premises licence application goes to the licensing authority (usually your district council) and also to the Police, Fire Service, Planning Department, Environmental Health Department, Child Protection Service and Trading Standards Service. So if you are not compliant in any area, this process may mean that you need to incur costs in putting things right.

MOVES TO CONTROL EXCESSIVE DRINKING

It is also worth noting that, in the last few years, the government has brought in more guidelines and mandatory codes of conduct for licensees aimed at curbing 'binge drinking' and anti-social behaviour. As with most such well meaning efforts by the government to control behaviour, these often have unintended consequences.

At the time of writing (August 2010), for example, the government had just started a consultation on options to implement its pledge to stop the sale of alcohol at below cost. The intention is to stop loss-leading supermarket promotions of lager, beer and cider which result in binge-drinking (and, incidentally, have contributed to the widespread closure of pubs). However, if not implemented sensibly with appropriate limits or exceptions, this could be highly damaging. A B&B giving a glass of wine on arrival, for instance, is serving alcohol at below cost – though not in a way that would encourage anti-social drinking. The tourism and hospitality industry, including the Bed and Breakfast Association, will be lobbying hard to ensure that normal B&B trading practices are not made illegal alongside the practices the new regulation is aimed at.

9
COMPLYING WITH FIRE REGULATIONS

England and Wales

Fire regulations are another area where the whole regulatory regime has changed in recent years. Whereas the new Licensing Act 2003 came in on 24 November 2005, the Fire Precautions Act 1971 was superseded by the Regulatory Reform (Fire Safety) Order (RRFSO) on 1 October 2006. The RRFSO potentially became the most serious threat to many B&B owners in England and Wales in recent years (the order does not apply to Scotland and Northern Ireland).

We spent a lot of time getting to grips with the nitty-gritty of the fire regulations from 2005, having had to invest heavily in upgrading our own B&B to meet the requirements of the local fire department (while also satisfying the planning and listed buildings departments). So we are able to give readers of this book a very practical perspective. More importantly, David, in his position of Chief Executive of the Bed and Breakfast Association has taken a key role in the hospitality industry in tackling the problems that arose in the first couple of years or so of the RRFSO. So in this Second Edition we are able to give a very comprehensive overview of the 2006 regulations and their effect.

This saga had echoes for David from the past. His grandparents had started and run a 57-bedroom hotel on Brighton seafront for many years and, as a boy, David occasionally helped out. He remembers the consternation when the Fire Precautions Act 1971 came in and the huge cost, uncertainty and disruption as hotels grappled with the Act's then onerous-seeming requirements. Much the same reaction was felt by small B&Bs in 2006 onwards as the RRFSO for the first time brought them into the enforcement regime alongside hotels.

FIRE CERTIFICATES

In a nutshell, the situation under the 1971 Act imposed the requirement for a fire certificate on buildings falling into clear (if perhaps arbitrary) criteria. As far as B&Bs are concerned, the relevant part was that, if you had no more than six letting rooms *and* no letting rooms above the first floor or below the ground floor, you did not need a fire certificate. It was as simple as that. (In recent years, if building works are carried out in private dwellings and the building has a second floor, under building regulations it must be provided with a 'protected means of escape', which may require fire doors to be installed.)

This had been the situation for many years, and so a huge number of B&Bs, probably the majority, had not had to worry about meeting the strict requirements of a fire certificate – those that have (like ourselves with our own B&B), have been forced quickly to become experts. They have had to grapple with the often-conflicting requirements of the fire and planning departments (if your building is listed like ours, a further dimension is added to the nightmare) and, above all, to come to realise how expensive it can be to adapt their property.

RRFSO

The RRFSO was supposedly intended by the government to be a deregulatory measure, lightening the burden on the industry, but most B&B owners (who had not been consulted) did not see it that way. In essence, it removes the old clear distinction between buildings requiring a fire certificate and buildings which do not need one. In fact, it abolishes the concept of fire certificates. The new regulations impose a responsibility on every individual property owner (including every B&B owner regardless of how many rooms they have or on which floors) to carry out a fire risk assessment and then to put 'reasonable and practicable' fire precautions in place 'where necessary'.

The new regime is intended to be no more nor less onerous that the one it replaced. In the words of the government department responsible (then the ODPM, Office of the Deputy Prime Minister, now DCLG, Department of Communities and Local Government):

the regime … promotes the avoidance of fires and mitigation of the effects of fires to a level equal to the current position of securing safe escape.

The new regime was not expected to prevent anyone from carrying out their business or, as the ODPM put it:

none of the proposals … would prevent any person from continuing to exercise any right or freedom which he or she might reasonably be expected to continue to exercise (Statement from the ODPM on the RRFSO, clause 333, 19 April 2004).

It is also important to note – and in the First Edition of this book we said 'we hope that the enforcing authorities will also note this' – that the fire precautions to be required are reasonable for the size of business. Again, to quote the ODPM directly:

Article 11 requires the responsible person [e.g. the B&B owner] [to make] 'such arrangements [i.e. fire precautions] as are appropriate, having regard to the size of his undertaking and the nature of its activities.

This is emphasised further in clause 339 of the ODPM's statement of 19 April 2004:

The overall effect of the provisions is to ensure that the [owner] is only required to take measures which are necessary to ensure the safety of relevant persons [read: paying guests and family] and hence ensures that the burdens [imposed by the new regulations] are proportionate to the benefits.

The following summary was published by the ODPM on the new regime:

The main effect of the changes will be a move towards greater emphasis on fire prevention in all non-domestic premises, including the voluntary sector and self-employed people with premises separate from their homes.

Fire certificates will be abolished and will cease to have legal status.

The Fire Safety Order … will apply in England and Wales. (Northern Ireland and Scotland will have their own laws.) It covers 'general fire precautions' and other fire safety duties which are needed to protect 'relevant persons' in case of fire in and around most 'premises'. The order requires fire precautions to be put in place 'where necessary' and to the extent that it is reasonable and practicable in the circumstances of the case.

Responsibility for complying with the Fire Safety Order rests with the 'responsible person'. In a workplace, this is the employer and any other person who may have control of any part of the premises, e.g. the occupier or owner. In all other premises the person or people in control of the premises will be responsible. If there is more than one responsible person in any type of premises, all must take all reasonable steps to work with each other.

If you are the responsible person you must carry out a fire risk assessment *which must focus on the safety in case of fire of all 'relevant persons'. It should pay particular attention to those at special risk, such as the disabled and those with special needs, and must include consideration of any dangerous substance likely to be on the premises. Your fire risk assessment will help you identify risks that can be removed or reduced and to decide the nature and extent of the general fire precautions you need to take to protect people against the fire risks that remain.*

If you employ five or more people you must record the significant findings of the assessment.

The enforcing bodies are the local fire and rescue authorities, of which there are 59 in the UK (50 in England and Wales). This made us worry that, in practice, the regulations would be interpreted and enforced very differently in different areas. Here, at least the regulations provided (in Article 26(2)) 'a mechanism for ensuring that enforcing authorities take a consistent approach to enforcement across England and Wales'.

In the First Edition, we said our view was that this new 'risk assessment' based regime would be:

☐ highly confusing, at least at first;

☐ disproportionately onerous on many small B&Bs which have so far fallen outside the fire certificate requirement of the 1971 Act;

☐ an unpleasant shock for many existing B&B owners who are unaware of its ramifications and have not been consulted; and

☐ a consultant's charter, ensuring many new advisers will spring up to charge property owners for doing fire risk assessments. Some of these will no doubt be of dubious qualification and/or will overcharge worried B&B owners.

We also worried that one effect would be that many small B&Bs, particularly those in very old or unusual buildings, will simply decide to close rather than face the consequences of the new regime. This would be a great pity, not only for those people deprived of their businesses but also for the British tourism industry which will lose 'bedstock' and, more importantly, individuality, quality and choice.

'Time will tell!' we said then – and now, four years later, we can tell you what happened. Unfortunately, many of our fears about enforcement were justified but, fortunately, thanks to a big campaign led by the Bed and Breakfast Association who created the 'Fire Safety SENSE Campaign' (www.firesafetysense.com), new government guidance was issued by both the Westminster and Edinburgh governments, and senior fire officers were made aware of concerns and have taken some corrective action.

ALARM BELL

Don't re-creosote the shed, strip paint off the dresser, burn rubbish in the garden or cook fish or curry as guests arrive. Smell is a powerful sense, hard-wired in the brain to emotional response. Try creating evocative aromas with flowers, beeswax polish, pot-pourri, coffee or baking bread. It will make a difference to your guests' reactions.

Figures released by the Scottish government in November 2009, when it published its own revised guidance for B&Bs (see below) (responding to industry concerns highlighted by the Bed and Breakfast Association's campaign), put the total additional 'unnecessary' cost burden in Scotland alone at an average of £14,286 per B&B business, which equates to a total unnecessary cost burden of £100 million in Scotland on the Scottish government's own figures as a result of the disproportionate enforcement of fire regulations on small B&Bs.

If the Scottish government's figures (the only cost burden estimates released by any national government) are a reasonable estimate for England and Wales too, the total unnecessary additional cost burden on the UK's 30,000 B&B businesses after 2006 would have been £428 million, or one fifth of the total gross turnover of the sector. If anything vindicates the association's urgent message to both governments since 2006 that the burden we were faced with was disproportionate, these figures certainly do.

The UK government's revised guidance for small B&Bs, *Do You Have Paying Guests?*, is available from the Department for Communities and Local government at: www.communities.gov.uk/publications/fire/payingguests or free of charge to members of the Bed and Breakfast Association (www.BandBassociaton.org).

The Fire Safety Minister stated:

> *The booklet* [Do You Have Paying Guests?] *has, through CFOA* [Chief Fire Officers' Association] *involvement, the support of the Chief Fire Officers throughout England. It is our belief that this booklet will help embed a practical, common sense approach to the enforcement of the* [RRFSO regulations] *by Fire and Rescue Authorities.*

After the involvement of the Bed and Breakfast Association and other industry bodies in its drafting, *Do You Have Paying Guests?* is much more helpful to B&B owners than previous official government guidance. For instance, it specifically states the following:

> *If your premises are similar to a family home, the fire safety precautions you will need to take are likely to be simpler than those needed for larger premises with more complicated layouts and staff.*

> *In many cases, you should be able to buy fire safety products for use in small premises from local retailers, such as DIY stores. These are likely to be less expensive than fire safety products which have been designed for larger and more complicated premises.*

> *What you need will depend on your business and your premises. The law does not require any particular measures to be in place. What it does say is that you must adequately manage the overall risk.*

> *Premises similar to a family home (i.e. two or three storeys) are likely to need an automatic fire detection system that runs from the mains electricity (with battery back-up) and consists of interconnected detectors. Detectors will be needed in the staircase, corridors and bedrooms. This (technically known as a Grade D LD2 system) has been designed for domestic premises. In the very smallest accommodation (no more than two storeys) which only has two or three guest bedrooms and short travel distances to a safe place outside, a connected system of detectors with a 10-year battery, or radio interlinked detectors may be good enough. (Technically, this is known as a Grade F LD2 system). You may be able to fit a Grade F system yourself.*

On emergency lighting, the booklet states:

If a fire knocks out the normal inside lighting, you should think about whether any 'borrowed lighting', for example from nearby street lamps, would be enough to allow people on the premises to find their way out. If not, it may be acceptable, in small premises, to rely on rechargeable torches which come on automatically if the main supply fails. You should have one in each room with a sign that says what they are for.

On fire-fighting equipment, the booklet states:

One extinguisher on each floor near the stairs and a fire blanket in the kitchen should be enough in most small premises.

On fire escape signs, the government guidance for small B&Bs is:

Signs are only required where they are needed. In small premises the escape route and the front door are likely to be obvious, so there may not be a need for emergency exit signs.

On doors, the guidance is:

You should keep all doors which open on to escape routes closed, especially at night. This is very important in the kitchen. If you leave doors open, it is less likely you will escape safely, even if the room has a fire detector. Although self-closing devices are a good way to make sure doors are closed, they can impact on the appearance and affect how you use the premises. If you decide these would be unsuitable, 'in-frame closers' or rising-butt hinges may be acceptable alternatives. Doors need to be strong enough to hold back smoke and fire long enough to give you time to escape. For small premises, a reasonably solid timber door that fits well into its frame is likely to be good enough. Any internal hollow 'egg-box'-type door would not offer adequate protection and should be replaced. Exit doors, such as the front or back door, should always be easy to unlock and must not need a key to unlock from the inside. A simple Yale-type latch or thumb turn is usually good enough.

As you may have already concluded from these quotations, the official UK guidance for small B&Bs is now considerably more sensible and proportionate than the precautions which many fire officers had been demanding of some B&Bs before this new guidance was produced with the involvement of the Bed and Breakfast Association.

In 2009 and 2010 since *Do You Have Paying Guests?* was introduced in England and Wales, there seem to have been far fewer instances of disproportionate enforcement action on small B&Bs. Indeed, some fire authorities withdrew enforcement notices they had issued based on the previous guidance. So the signs have been encouraging that the Bed and Breakfast Association's campaign has made a real change in enforcement.

Scotland

In Scotland, the RRFSO does not apply. The equivalent legislation was the Fire (Scotland) Act 2005. However, a very similar set of problems to those in England and Wales quickly arose in Scotland – inconsistent, over-zealous and disproportionate enforcement. The original Scottish guidelines on fire precautions also quickly proved to be inappropriate and unduly onerous where small B&Bs are concerned. The Bed and Breakfast Association's 'Fire Safety SENSE Campaign' highlighted concerns that previous fire safety requirements were complex and prohibitively expensive.

New fire safety guidance for Scotland published in June 2010 is set to reduce the financial and administrative burden on Scotland's estimated 7,000 B&B and self-catering businesses by an average of £14,286 each – a total reduction in the cost burden on small accommodation businesses in Scotland of £100 million, on the Scottish government's own figures.

The new guidance (*Practical Fire Safety Guidance for Small Bed & Breakfast and Self-catering Premises*) was developed by the Scottish government to 'directly address these concerns' and will 'maintain fire safety levels while reducing the average investment in safety equipment by over 90 per cent'. The new guidance will also ensure that all fire safety requirements are now applied 'consistently as well as proportionately to the size of property'.

The Scottish Government Minister for Community Safety Fergus Ewing said:

> *The Scottish government has listened at length to business owners' concerns and proposed a solution that reduces red tape and reduces cost while ensuring their paying guests are safe from the ever-present risk of fire.*

An independent analysis has calculated the average cost of compliance under the new guidance to be £1,090 per B&B – a saving of over £13,000 compared with the previous guidance – according to the figures published by the Scottish government. For more detail, see www.infoscotland.com/firelaw. Click on 'Sector Specific Guidance' and look for B&Bs.

10
OBEYING FOOD SAFETY REQUIREMENTS

This is yet another area where it is not just common sense you need to follow but a swathe of regulation, overseen by bureaucracy. And again, as with fire regulations, the whole regime changed in 2006 when the UK implemented the EU Food Hygiene Regulations. This covers all 'food business operators', which include *all* B&Bs because they serve breakfast.

The key requirements are as follows:

☐ **Registration**: you need to register with the 'competent authority' – in the case of B&Bs this means your local environmental health officer (EHO). For the vast majority of B&Bs, this will be entirely new. The process of applying for a licence involves a submission to the local EHO, but unlicensed B&Bs (the vast majority, of course) will not have had any contact with their EHO unless they have had an inspection visit.

The regulations go further in the case of food businesses dealing with 'produce of animal origin'. Such businesses are required to be approved before they start trading. Although the regulations state that they are not permitted to trade after 1 January without official approval, the transitional arrangements indicate that either conditional or full approval will be granted at the next scheduled visit from your EHO. In the mean time the business owner need take no action as the initiative lies with the EHO. At the time of writing it is not clear whether B&Bs will fall into this category of business – a literal reading of the regulations would suggest they would, by virtue of serving, say, bacon and sausages (not to mention dairy products). Against this it is not obvious why a B&B should be treated in the same category as an abattoir or a meat-packing plant.

☐ **Food safety**: the food you serve must be safe. There is not much we can add here!

☐ **Traceability**: you must know where your foods have come from. For a B&B, this requirement should be met by keeping receipts, which you will be doing anyway in order to claim food costs in your accounts.

☐ **Risk assessment**: you must have carried out a risk assessment to ensure that you are complying with microbiological criteria, temperature requirements and general hygiene good practice – but here the regulations make allowances for some small businesses.

☐ **HACCP**: you must have a food safety management system in place based on Hazard Analysis and Critical Control Points (HACCP) principles. See our website at www.howtorunabandb.com for further information, links, etc.

All this looks daunting, but most food safety practice comes down to basic principles such as using safe ingredients, following use-by dates, storing food at the right temperature, storing cooked meats on a separate shelf from raw meats (with cooked meats above), cooking food through properly and preparing food in clean conditions. Most competent cooks will have no problems with any of this. The difference when you run a B&B is that, now you are running a 'food business', you not only have to follow good practice but also have to be able to demonstrate that you are doing so. This means recording your policies to show 'due diligence' to your EHO.

The key question in food safety practice is: can you demonstrate *that your food is* safe *for anyone who may eat it?*

All food businesses, irrespective of their nature and size, must comply with what the regulations call the 'prerequisite requirements'. These include:

☐ safe handling

☐ raw materials

☐ waste

☐ pest control

☐ sanitation

☐ water quality

☐ cold chain

☐ potential allergens

☐ training

☐ traceability.

As a general rule, the need for HACCP-related record keeping should be well balanced and can be limited to what is essential for food safety. This means that a diary which shows when things went wrong (and how they were corrected), rather than copious records of day-to-day routines, would be all that would be required. The following guidance (*Food Hygiene: A Guide for Businesses*) is published by the Food Standards Agency (FSA):

Food safety management procedures

You must put in place 'food safety management procedures' based on the principles of HACCP (hazard analysis critical control point). You must also:

- *keep these in place permanently*

- *keep up-to-date documents and records relating to your procedures*

- *review your procedures if you change what you produce or how you work*

In practice, this means that you must have procedures in place to manage food safety 'hazards' in your business. This is similar to the previous legal requirements, but you must now write these procedures down, update them as needed and keep records that can be checked by your local authority.

The regulations are designed to be flexible, so these procedures can be in proportion to the size of your business and the type of work you do. This means that many small businesses will be able to have very simple procedures and simple records.

General requirements

You must keep your premises clean and maintained in good repair and condition.

The layout, design, construction, site and size of your premises must:

- *allow adequate maintenance, cleaning and/or disinfection*

- *avoid or minimise air-borne contamination (i.e. contamination carried in the air)*

- *provide enough working space for you to carry out all tasks hygienically*

- *protect against the build-up of dirt, contact with toxic materials, shedding of particles into food and forming of condensation or mould on surfaces*

- *allow good food hygiene practices, including protection against contamination and, in particular, pest control*

- *provide, where necessary, suitable conditions for handling and storing food while keeping it at appropriate temperatures, designed to allow those temperatures to be monitored and, where necessary, recorded*

Handwashing facilities and toilets

You must have an adequate number of flush lavatories, connected to an effective drainage system.

Toilets must not open directly into rooms where you handle food.

You must have an adequate number of washbasins, suitably located and used only for cleaning hands.

Washbasins for cleaning hands must have hot and cold running water, and materials for cleaning hands and for hygienic drying.

Where necessary, you should have a separate sink for washing food.

Ventilation

You must have enough ventilation, either natural (e.g. opening windows or vents) or mechanical (e.g. extractor fans).

Ventilation systems must be constructed to allow access to clean or replace filters and other parts.

Toilets must have enough ventilation, either natural or mechanical.

Other requirements

You must have adequate lighting, either natural (daylight) and/or artificial (electric light).

Drainage facilities must be adequate for the purpose intended. They must be designed and constructed to avoid the risk of contamination.

You must provide adequate facilities for staff to change their clothes, where necessary.

You must not store cleaning chemicals and disinfectants in areas where food is handled.

Rooms where food is prepared, treated or processed

There are special requirements for rooms where you prepare, treat or process food. These do not include dining rooms. The design and layout of the room must allow good food hygiene practices, including protection against contamination between and during tasks.

Surfaces

Surfaces (including surfaces of equipment) in areas where food is handled, particularly those that are touched by food, must be maintained in a sound condition and be easy to clean and, where necessary, to disinfect.

This means that surfaces need to be made of materials that are smooth, washable, corrosion-resistant and non-toxic, unless you can satisfy your local authority that other materials are appropriate.

Washing equipment and food

You must have adequate facilities, where necessary, for cleaning, disinfecting and storing utensils and equipment.

These facilities need to be made of corrosion-resistant materials, be easy to clean and have an adequate supply of hot and cold water.

You must have adequate facilities, where necessary, for washing food. Every sink (or other facilities) for washing food must have an adequate supply of hot and/or cold water. The water must be 'potable' (drinking quality). These facilities must be kept clean and, where necessary, disinfected.

Personal hygiene

Every person working in a food-handling area must maintain a high level of personal cleanliness. He or she must wear suitable, clean clothing and, where necessary, protective clothing.

Handwashing

Effective handwashing is extremely important to help prevent harmful bacteria from spreading from people's hands to food, work surfaces, equipment etc. Make sure that all staff that work with food wash their hands properly:

- *when entering the food handling area, e.g. after a break*

- *or going to the toilet*

- *before preparing food*

- *after touching raw food, such as meat/poultry and eggs*

- *after handling food waste or emptying a bin*

- *after cleaning*

- *after blowing their nose.*

Don't forget that staff should dry hands thoroughly on a disposable towel – harmful bacteria can spread more easily if your hands are wet or damp.

Foods

You must not accept raw materials or ingredients, or any other material used in processing products, if they are known to be, or might reasonably be expected to be, contaminated in a way that means the final product would be unfit for human consumption.

You must store raw materials and all ingredients in appropriate conditions, designed to prevent harmful deterioration and protect them from contamination.

At all stages of production, processing and distribution, you must protect food against any contamination likely to make it unfit for human consumption, harmful to health or contaminated in a way that means it would be unreasonable to expect it to be eaten in that state.

You must have adequate procedures to control pests and to prevent domestic animals (pets) from getting into places where food is prepared, handled or stored. If your local authority permits domestic animals, in special cases, you must have adequate procedures to prevent this from causing contamination.

Hazardous and/or inedible substances must be adequately labelled and stored in separate and secure containers.

You also need to make sure that the food you make or sell complies with specific 'micro-biological criteria'. These criteria put limits on the levels of certain bacteria that are allowed to be in foods. In practice, most small catering businesses and small food shops may not need to do any testing of the levels of bacteria in the food they make or sell. But you must be able to show that you have suitable food safety management procedures in place that control the levels of bacteria in food.

Temperature

You must not keep foods at temperatures that might cause a risk to health.

The 'cold chain' must not be interrupted for foods that rely on temperature control for their safety. However, you are allowed to have foods outside temperature control for limited periods of time to allow you to prepare, transport, store, display and serve food, as long as this does not cause a risk to health.

Enforcement of the law

Local authorities are responsible for enforcing food hygiene laws. To do this, enforcement officers may visit your business premises to inspect them. These officers might come on a routine inspection, or they might visit because of a complaint.

They have the right to enter and inspect your premises at any reasonable time and will usually come without telling you first.

What help can I get?

If you would like advice about obeying food hygiene law, get in touch with your local authority.

If you run a small catering business, there are packs available to help you put in place food safety management procedures based on the principles of HACCP. These packs have been produced by the FSA in England, Scotland and Northern Ireland, and by local authorities in Wales.

England

'Safer food, better business', an innovative and practical approach to food safety management, has been developed by the FSA in partnership with small catering businesses and more than 50 local authorities. If you would like to order a copy of 'Safer food, better business' contact FSA publications ... You can view it online at www.food.gov.uk

Wales

Several local authorities have previously developed guidance packs on HACCP for caterers and FSA Wales has encouraged the sharing of these packs throughout Welsh local authorities. Businesses should contact their local authority for more information.

Scotland

FSA Scotland has drawn on expertise from the food industry including small businesses, local authorities and the Scottish Food Advisory Committee to develop a HACCP-based system called 'CookSafe'. This is also available in Chinese, Urdu and Punjabi. Businesses that would like a copy should contact their local authority. You can view it online at www.food.gov.uk

Northern Ireland

FSA Northern Ireland has produced guidance for the catering sector called 'Safe Catering', working with caterers and local authorities. This guidance, which has been developed and refined over a number of years, is widely accepted by the catering sector in Northern Ireland. Businesses should contact their local authority for information.

Guidance documents

The FSA has also produced guidance documents on the new regulations, which you can read on www.food.gov.uk

FSA publications

There are a number of FSA publications that you might find helpful. These include:

- *Food Hygiene – A Guide for Businesses*

- *Starting up – Your First Steps to Running a Catering Business*

- *Food Law Inspections and Your Business*

- *Eggs – What Caterers Need to Know.*

HACCP food safety checklist

Subject	Yes	Date
Has anything changed since you last went through this list?	❑	......
Have you written down your safety procedures?	❑	......
Do you carry out a regular review of your systems?	❑	......
Are you confident about the 4 'Cs' – Cross-contamination; Cleaning; Chilling; Cooking?	❑	......
Do you have a system for dealing with complaints?	❑	......
Do you have a system of traceability of products?	❑	......
If something went wrong, could you say where you got all your supplies from?	❑	......
Do you know what allergens your food may contain?	❑	......
Does your kitchen have adequate ventilation?	❑	......
Are the kitchen walls, floors and ceilings in good repair and washable?	❑	......
Do you have a hand wash basin in a convenient place?	❑	......

Do you have adequate storage for waste and in the right place? ❏ ......

If you have staff, do they really know what cross-contamination is and how to prevent it? ❏ ......

If you have staff, have they received appropriate training? ❏ ......

Do you keep a record of staff training? ❏ ......

Are your hygiene rules written down so your staff can refresh their memories? ❏ ......

Do you keep staff sickness records? ❏ ......

Do you ask new staff to complete an 'employee medical questionnaire' to ensure they are fit to work in a food preparation environment? ❏ ......

Do you have a system for staff to tell you about any illness? ❏ ......

Do you have a first-aid kit properly stocked? ❏ ......

Does your stock rotation system work effectively? ❏ ......

Do you know the temperatures at which different foods should be stored? ❏ ......

Can you demonstrate that your fridges and freezers are keeping to the right temperatures? ❏ ......

Do you have separate areas for storing raw and cooked foods? ❏ ......

How often do you check your fridge/freezer temperatures? ❏ ......

Do you have written procedures to define cooking/reheating times? ❏ ......

Do you (and your staff if applicable) know what temperature will kill most bacteria? ❏ ......

Can you demonstrate that temperatures are accurate? ❏ ......

Are you aware of the potential dangers of cooking or reheating in a microwave oven? ❏ ......

Do you have rules for cooling food after cooking? ❏ ......

Can you demonstrate that your cooling times are right? ❏ ......

Are you sure there could be no cross-contamination during cooling? ❏ ......

Do you have a reliable system for establishing the 'shelf life' of foods once they have been cooked? ❏ ......

Can you demonstrate that the way you handle and prepare food will prevent cross-contamination? ❑ ......

Do you have separate equipment for raw and cooked foods? ❑ ......

Do you have a safe system for defrosting foods? ❑ ......

Do you know at what temperature you should 'hot-hold' food? ❑ ......

Do you check and record your 'hot-holding' temperatures? ❑ ......

Do you have a cleaning routine? ❑ ......

Can you demonstrate that your staff keep to the cleaning routine? ❑ ......

Are you sure you use the right chemicals at the right temperatures and for the right times for effective cleaning? ❑ ......

Do you store your cleaning materials in a safe area away from foods? ❑ ......

If you use a dishwasher, do you know what its operating temperature is? ❑ ......

Do you use bacterial wipes – especially on your temperature probe? ❑ ......

Can you demonstrate that you regularly check for any contamination? ❑ ......

Is your kitchen properly pest-proof? ❑ ......

Do you have a system for checking evidence of pests? ❑ ......

Are your fly screens fitted properly? ❑ ......

Do you use a pest control contractor? ❑ ......

Can you demonstrate that you have identified any critical points in your procedures and have set limits for them? ❑ ......

Can you demonstrate that your staff are carrying out all the necessary hygiene procedures and checks even when you are not there? ❑ ......

Can you demonstrate that you have taken the right corrective action whenever something has gone wrong? ❑ ......

If you are confident, then sign and date here to say you have considered all the questions.

Signature......................... Date.......................

11
FURTHER LEGISLATION

Complying with disability regulations

DISABILITY DISCRIMINATION ACT (DDA) 1995/2005

This Act gives disabled people rights in certain areas, including access to goods, facilities and services. This includes B&Bs. You are required to make *reasonable* adjustments to the way you deliver your services and to the physical features of your premises to make it easier for disabled guests to use them.

As a service provider, you need to make sure you treat disabled guests in the same way as you treat other guests, unless there is adequate justification for less favourable treatment, such as health and safety. You would be treating guests with disabilities less favourably if you:

☐ refuse to serve them;

☐ offer less favourable terms; or

☐ offer a lower standard of service compared with what you normally offer.

If you treat someone less favourably, the Act allows them to seek damages from you through the county court.

Since 1 October 2004, service providers have had a duty to take *reasonable* steps to remove, alter or avoid any physical barriers that make it impossible or unreasonably difficult for disabled people to make full use of facilities, if the service cannot be provided by an alternative method.

Note that you are only required to do what is *reasonable*. The Equalities and Human Rights Commission (EHRC)'s Code of Practice gives more information on assessing whether a particular adjustment is reasonable. In general, the factors to consider would include whether:

☐ the proposed adjustment would meet the needs of the disabled person;

☐ the adjustment is affordable; and

☐ the adjustment would have a serious effect on other people.

The Act permits service providers to justify less favourable treatment (and in some instances failure to make a reasonable adjustment) when there is no possibility to do so, despite the fact that this would mean that a disabled person is treated less favourably. Service providers do, therefore, have flexibility when considering how to make their services accessible to disabled people. Remember that what might be considered reasonable for a national hotel chain may not be so for a small B&B or guesthouse.

ACCESS STATEMENTS

The DDA recommends that you produce an access statement, and this has now also been made a condition of approval for a star rating under the VisitBritain quality inspection scheme.

There is a useful Help section about access statements, including background information, guidance and a template, at VisitBritain's website www.VisitBritain.com/accessstatements

Besides the cost of making physical alterations, there may be other restrictions – for instance, those imposed by the 'listing' authorities on what changes are allowed for listed buildings.

EQUALITY ACT 2010

From 1 October 2010, the majority of The Equality Act 2010 was implemented and this replaces major parts of the provisions of the Disability Discrimination Act. The Equality Act is intended:

to provide a new legislative framework to protect the rights of individuals and advance equality of opportunity for all; to update, simplify and strengthen the previous legislation; and to deliver a simple, modern and accessible framework of discrimination law which protects individuals from unfair treatment and promotes a fair and more equal society.

The provisions in the Equality Act will come into force at different times to allow for the people and organisations affected by the new laws to prepare for them. The government is currently considering how the different provisions will be commenced so that the Act is implemented in an effective and proportionate way.

The smoking 'ban' (2007)

Since the First Edition of this book, in 2007, the smoking regulations came in, making smoking in all enclosed public places illegal. Since by now this is so well known we need not say much about it, beyond saying that as far as B&Bs are concerned, this means no smoking in any shared areas while guests are staying – e.g. corridors, lounge, dining room, etc. However, guests' own bedrooms are *not* considered public places for this purpose, so you can (if you wish) allow guests to smoke in their own bedrooms. This means that you are free to designate any room(s) as 'smoking' rooms if you want. It is up to you. Clearly if you do not designate any of your rooms as 'smoking' rooms, guests are not allowed to smoke at all at your B&B (except outside, in the garden).

Data Protection Act 1998

Data protection is outside the remit of this book other than to note that if you compile a computer-based list of customer and/or inquirer details, the Data Protection Act (DPA) lays down rules covering how you are allowed to use the data. Most B&Bs who simply contact past customers who have given them their details to let them know about special offers or prices should not need to worry about this. However, if you plan to mail or email lists of potential customers, do be aware of the DPA's requirements. For further information, see the Information Commissioner's Office website at www.ico.gov.uk

Discriminating on the basis of age

Despite the last (Labour) government's talk about not adding new burdens to those already suffered by small businesses, their actions are the opposite: new red tape continued to rumble inexorably from the Westminster pipeline.

Many accommodation businesses restrict availability based on age. Many B&Bs and holiday cottage owners, for instance, refuse bookings from same-sex groups under 25. Such a rule is simple, easy to understand and enforce, and probably generally achieves its aim of preventing hire by the sort of groups that the owner knows from experience are likely to cause damage, problems with neighbours, etc. The Labour government's Equality Office, however, proposed in 2009 to abolish the freedom of owners to discriminate in this way.

These type of rules – there are, of course, may other examples – are simply a result of owners or service providers exercising their freedom to limit their own service in certain ways. Common sense recognises this and sees an appropriate balance of freedoms and no real 'harm' (to use the word in the consultation document) done in such cases – indeed, vastly more harm prevented. In our experience, most people trying to book (say) a group of ten 19-year-old men into a holiday home for a stag weekend are not the slightest bit surprised that many owners do not want such a group, and know only too well why! The government did not, calling it a 'stereotypical assumption'.

Smile and be unfailingly friendly, courteous, thoughtful and helpful. Too easy? It's so rarely done, it'll put you miles ahead of most of the British hospitality industry even if you slip up in other areas.

We can see no public benefit in removing the freedom of property owners and service providers in this way and believe that the proposed legislation is not based on evidence or on the prevention of 'harm' (the government's word), but purely on the ideology of equality. Thus the consultation document even sees a simple rule imposed by car-hire companies (because of insurance) limiting car hire to under to under 75-year-olds as an attack on equality and as enforcing negative stereotypes.

The Labour government seemed to accept the industry's argument to provide an exemption for age-related holidays (e.g. Saga and Club 18–30) but it did not accept the argument that accommodation providers should be able to apply age restrictions on the use of their property. The consultation document referred dismissively to the concerns the industry has raised as 'anecdotal evidence … compounded by stereotypical assumptions'.

This whole area may be up for some changes – at least in emphasis, priority and appetite for enforcement – after the change of government. We can only watch and wait. For further information see www.equalities.gov.uk

Providing Internet access for guests

Again, this strays outside the book's remit, but the Digital Economy Bill seems set to make changes which would affect B&Bs and guest houses. As part of trying to counter illegal file-sharing and copyright theft, there are proposals that Internet service providers (ISPs) should be made responsible for such offences being committed by users of their connections. Again, the law of unintended consequences kicks in: ISPs also include B&Bs offering WiFi connections to guests (whether free or paid for). This is another lobbying priority for the Bed and Breakfast Association and the Tourism Alliance. The aim is to convince Parliament either to exclude small B&Bs from a definition of ISPs or to find a low-cost and practical way that such ISPs cannot be unfairly held responsible for something they have no control over.

12
MANAGING YOUR FINANCES

Accounting and tax are closely related areas and both are 'musts' – you *must* produce accounts, even if only for your benefit, and you *must* pay tax. Having said that, there are different ways you can account and pay tax on a small B&B business.

Keeping accounts

WHY KEEP ACCOUNTS?

If you have not run a business before, the thought of producing sets of accounts may well be daunting. Aren't there ways you can run a B&B without accounts? Well, yes – sort of. For a very small operation, the rent-a-room scheme (see below) allows a simplified way of paying tax without the Inland Revenue needing to see any accounts.

But – and this is a big but – you shouldn't be looking at ways to avoid doing any accounts. We say this not for the sake of the taxman or the accountancy profession, but for your sake as a business owner. Don't be scared of accounts – you need them!

BUDGETING

In Chapter 4 we talked about how essential budgeting is and how relatively simple it can be while still being invaluable. Budgets are the 'what if?', crystal-ball version of accounts.

Think of it as a mirror. In theory, if all goes to plan, your accounts should be identical to your budget. The one certainty is that they never will be – but that is not the point. The point is that budgeting is necessary to help you set your course, quantify your targets and maintain the discipline you need on costs, margins and sales.

For the same reasons, having put together a budget it would be nonsensical not to record the 'actuals' to see how you have done in relation to your targets. Those actuals are your accounts.

BEING REALISTIC

So you need accounts to manage your business long term as well as to satisfy the taxman. The discipline of producing accounts forces you to confront any self-delusions you may be clinging to about your business. We all do it. Businesspeople are human and usually passionate about their businesses, and so often have stubborn blind spots.

You may be sure that cutting your prices by 5% was the right decision – bookings went up, after all. But your accounts will show the reality of sales and profits in the cold, hard light of day. Sometimes it is uncomfortable – your pet theory may be proved wrong or your business may actually be less profitable than you thought while all the sales were coming in. But the alternative – blissful ignorance, steering the ship blindfold – is always worse.

WHEN YOU DECIDE TO SELL YOUR B&B

There is another good reason for keeping good accounts. As and when you decide to sell your B&B, your accounts may make a big difference to the price you can get. Think about it. What is a buyer buying, other than the physical property itself? What they are buying is a 'revenue stream', or the capacity of the business to generate money. This revenue-generating capacity is known by accountants as 'goodwill' – a homely sounding word but a vital one for any seller of a business.

It is the added value that you are in effect asking the buyer to pay you for. If they just have your word that you have been selling quite well for a few years, they are unlikely to pay much. If you have clear and well produced sets of accounts for each year you have been trading, backed up by bank records, receipts and invoices, then you have proved your sales and profits and thus can command an appropriate price for the goodwill in your business.

The best thing of all from your point of view is to have a set of successive accounts showing good, steady, consistent increases in sales and profits, because that demonstrates to a buyer that what they are paying for – which, after all, is the *future* of your business – is worth more than the present or the past. But more of that in Chapter 20, when we come to selling your B&B.

DECIDING ON YOUR ACCOUNTING SYSTEM

The two most common ways of accounting for B&Bs are as a sole trader business or under Her Majesty's Revenue and Customs' (HMRC – the new name for the Inland Revenue) 'Rent a Room' scheme.

The Rent a Room scheme

The Rent a Room scheme is suitable for small-scale B&B businesses. Basically you can receive up to £4,250 B&B income a year tax free, but *you can't offset any costs against your income*. The following explanation of the scheme is from HMRC:

If you already have a lodger or are thinking about letting furnished rooms in your home, you can receive up to £4,250 a year tax-free (£2,150 if letting jointly). This is known as the Rent a Room scheme.

How the scheme works

The Rent a Room scheme is an optional exemption scheme that lets you receive a certain amount of tax-free 'gross' income (receipts before expenses) from renting furnished accommodation in your only or main home.

Who can take advantage of the scheme?

You can choose to take advantage of the scheme if you let furnished accommodation in your only or family home to a lodger. (Your only or family home is the one where you/your family live for most of the time. A lodger is someone who pays to live in your home, sometimes with meals provided, and who often shares the family rooms.)

A lodger can occupy a single room or an entire floor of your home. However, the scheme does not apply if your home is converted into separate flats that you rent out. In this case you will need to declare your rental income to HM Revenue & Customs (HMRC) and pay tax in the normal way. Nor does the scheme apply if you let unfurnished accommodation in your home.

Do you have to be a home owner?

No. You can choose to take advantage of the Rent a Room scheme, regardless of whether you are a home owner or are renting your home. However, if you are renting, you should check whether your lease allows you to take in a lodger.

If you're a mortgage payer it's best to check whether taking in a lodger is within your mortgage lender's and insurer's terms and conditions.

If you share a home and both let a room or rooms

If you and your spouse are both letting furnished accommodation in your joint home, you will each be entitled to receive half of the allowance (up to £2,125 for the 2010–11 tax year) without paying tax.

If you provide meals and laundry services and charge for such additional services, you will need to add the payments you receive to the rent, to work out the total receipts. If you get more than £4,250 a year in total, you will have to pay tax, even if the rent is less than that.

The advantages and disadvantages of the scheme

There are advantages and disadvantages of the scheme – it's simply a matter of working out what is best for you.

*The principal point to bear in mind is that if you are in the Rent a Room scheme **you can't claim any expenses relating to the letting** (for example, wear and tear, insurance, repairs, heating and lighting).*

To work out whether you will be better off joining the scheme or declaring all of your letting income and claiming expenses on your tax return you need to compare the following:

(a) how much income you are left with after your expenses, and

(b) the amount of your receipts (rent plus any income from laundry services, meals, etc.) over £4,250 or £2,125 if letting jointly (these figures are for the 2010–11 tax year).

If you opt out of the scheme (or simply do nothing) you will pay income tax on the first amount. If you opt into the scheme you will pay tax on the second amount.

HMRC publishes some example calculations to help you decide which method would be best for you [see www.howtorunabandb.com for links].

Rent a Room scheme and running a business

If you run a bed and breakfast business or a guest house, or provide catering and cleaning services as part of a letting business, the Rent a Room scheme can still apply to you. You will need to complete the relevant parts of the self-employment pages of your Self Assessment tax return.

How to opt in or out of the scheme

If you want to opt in, if you don't normally receive a tax return and your receipts are below the tax-free thresholds for the scheme, the tax exemption is automatic so you don't need to do anything. If you wish to opt in and your receipts are above the tax-free threshold, you must tell your tax office – you can do this by completing a tax return and claiming the allowance.

If you want to opt out, just complete a tax return within the usual deadline and declare the relevant lettings income and expenses on the property pages.

There are up-to-date links about the Rent a Room scheme on our website at www.howtorunabandb.com, or join the Bed and Breakfast Association (for more information, forms and links see www.bandbassociation.org).

Sole trader

If your B&B business will be on a significant scale and will be growing, you may well decide (as we did) that the Rent a Room scheme is not tax effective for you. In that case, the alternative is to account for the business normally as a sole trader. To do this you have to *register* your B&B business with your local tax office. You need to ring them up with your tax reference and NI number and give them the date your B&B business is due to start, or when it started if it has started already (but beware: you cannot register more than three months after your business has started, on pain of a £100 fine).

You then simply produce accounts for your B&B based on your actual income and costs, and submit them to HMRC as part of your tax return, by the 31 January following the end of each tax year (so, for the tax year 6 April 2010 to 5 April 2011, you must submit your tax return by 31 January 2012 with your remittance for the expected tax due). You will be charged tax on your profits, after taking into account any portion of your personal tax allowances which have not been used against other employment.

Be obsessive about keeping your receipts and invoices for every single B&B cost. These are your direct business costs, so every £1 spent on eggs, sausages or laundry is £1 taken off your taxable profits.

Although it will add to your costs, it is advisable (at least in your first year) to use an accountant to prepare your accounts and submit your tax return. Choose a friendly local accountant, not a big-name firm (which would be unnecessarily expensive), and ask them to give you a quote in advance.

The general overheads – i.e. the costs of gas, electricity, water rates, council tax (or business rates) and mortgage or property financing costs, etc. – should be allocated as business costs on a pro-rata basis to the floor area of your premises devoted to the B&B. If 30% of the property is guest bedrooms, guest breakfast room and other guest areas, then 30% of the property overheads will be applied in your B&B accounts as a business cost.

Dealing with VAT

Value added tax (VAT) is highly complex and outside the scope of this book, as currently the threshold for registration for VAT is £70,000. This means that you would only have to register for VAT, and hence charge VAT to customers, once your B&B turnover (total sales revenue) is above £70,000.

Because a three-bedroom B&B charging £65 per night would have to reach just over 98% occupancy year round to hit a £70,000 turnover, it is highly unlikely that most readers of this book will find that VAT is relevant to them. Again, this is something that you should discuss with an accountant.

Needless to say, you will not want to register for VAT until you have to because, although you would gain by being able to claim back VAT spend on business purchases, you would lose much more by effectively having to raise your prices by 17.5% (20% from 4 January 2011). In practice, this often means that you are forced to reduce your net room rate to mitigate the rise in the tax-inclusive price, *and* you suffer a loss of sales because of the forced price rise – a nasty 'double whammy'.

This unfair downside of VAT does at least give small B&Bs an advantage in competing with local hotels – they have to charge VAT, and you don't. Enjoy it while you can, as there are hardly any other advantages given to small businesses by government!

Arranging insurance

When you open up as a B&B, you need to change your insurance from a standard household-type policy to a specialist B&B or guest house insurance policy. There are a number of specialist insurers providing these policies, which give the usual family household and buildings cover and also additional cover for your public liability (e.g. for injury to paying guests) and even for (optionally) theft or malicious damage by paying guests.

Prices can vary hugely. On joining the Bed and Breakfast Association, B&B owners have reported savings of £400, £850 and even £1,400 in premium simply by checking the options the association gives to its members.

So our advice is do your homework, and shop around – get lots of quotes and ask lots of questions!

The 'bed tax' threat

This chapter on accounting and tax is perhaps the best place to mention yet another potential threat to B&Bs: a 'bed tax'. The decades-old debate on how local government in the UK is financed led to the last (Labour) government commissioning Sir Michael Lyons to produce a report on all the options. The 'Lyons Inquiry' issued its report in 2007.

The Lyons Inquiry stated that:

> *taxes on tourist activity have been suggested as a way of raising revenue for authorities, and ensuring that visitors contribute to the public services they use ... The most frequent proposal was for a local tax on hotel and similar accommodation.*

Sir Michael Lyons stated that he is 'interested in exploring this issue further, though I have noted that considerable further work would need to be undertaken if new forms of taxation were to be contemplated'.

Basically what this meant is that the government had identified the tourist industry – hotels and B&Bs – as a potential 'soft target' for yet another new tax. The reasoning was that, while people may squeal about their council tax bills, who will worry about a few pounds added to every night spent at a B&B or hotel? Travellers and tourists are good for a milking for extra revenue and don't command sympathy like pensioners or homeowners.

The authors, through their founding involvement in the Bed and Breakfast Association (BBA), have been close to the association's response to this very real threat to the future viability of B&Bs. We reproduce below an extract from the BBA's official submission to the Lyons Inquiry at its interim report and consultation stage, which is self-explanatory:

> *We believe that a tourist tax of the sort mooted in your report would be highly damaging to UK tourism, both inbound and domestic, and would be especially and dispropor-tionately damaging to the B&B sector; that such a tax would be counterproductive and would depress total tourism-related revenue to the exchequer more than the amount raised by the tax; and that the introduction of such a tax would result in the closure of significant numbers of B&B businesses, especially in rural areas with already weak economies ...*
>
> *Although the bed and breakfast sector is fragmented and consists of very small individual*

businesses, overall it forms a highly significant part of the UK's tourism bedstock; in 2003, stays at B&Bs represented 7% of stays and 8% of spending on domestic tourist stays by UK residents, compared to 29% of stays or 41% of spending being in hotels. So for every four hotel stays taken, there was one stay in a B&B in 2003. The stays in B&Bs represented £1.849 billion of tourism spend in the UK made by UK residents alone, a figure hugely increased once spend by foreign visitors to UK B&Bs are added (UK Tourism Survey).

The above figures underestimate the relative importance of the B&B sector in rural areas, where a higher proportion of bedstock will be represented by B&Bs as compared with hotels. In many of the UK's most sparsely populated and economically weak areas, the only accommodation available is in the B&B sector as many such areas would not commercially support hotels. The B&Bs in these areas will tend to be the most economically fragile, therefore the most likely to close as a result of any negative impact to the B&B sector. Thus any such impact will disproportionately affect such rural areas ...

Because the hotels sector is almost entirely operated using specialised IT-based booking systems, whereas the B&B sector is almost entirely operated by manual booking systems, a tourist tax would cause a huge new burden on the B&B sector, many times more onerous than its impact on the hotels sector. For the first time, B&B owners would have to create reporting systems specifically to cope with such a tax. Many have indicated to us that this alone would be sufficient to cause them to consider closure.

As B&Bs have no statutory registration system, any new tourist tax would effectively create a new national registration and regulatory system for B&Bs, requiring a new national database of B&Bs and all the requisite monitoring and administration this requires, which would in itself be a disproportionate cost to government compared with the amounts of tax raised from B&Bs (especially if the reduction in other taxes, including income tax, resulting from a new tourist tax is taken into account).

The B&B sector ... has [recently] suffered very considerable cost increases and administrative burdens, often disproportionately compared with the economy generally. These are already tipping the fragile economic balance of many B&B businesses towards closure; if in addition, a new tourist tax were imposed ... the result would be that thousands of B&Bs would decide to close.

We would also make some wider points about a tourist tax: the UK already applies 17.5% VAT to accommodation and other tourist services, compared with say 5.5% in France (a major competitor for inbound tourism revenue), and about 8.5% on average in the EU for accommodation. The UK also lacks the financial support offered by *governments in many of our competitor countries for small-scale tourist accommodation in rural areas (for example, in converted agricultural buildings). The UK already overtaxes tourism spend compared with our key competitors.*

We would also make a wider strategic and environmental point about the usage of existing buildings in the UK. The B&B sector represents a very efficient and sustainable usage of the UK's building stock, as it effectively represents a subsidy by the residential sector of tourist accommodation. Were this sector to be even further penalised by additional taxation and administrative burdens, the effect would be either to (a) reduce available tourism bedstock and hence damage the UK's £74 billion tourism economy, and/or (b) require replacement purpose-built commercial bedstock, and thus more new building, reduced sustainability, more damage to the environment, less open land, more usage of energy and other resources, and the under-usage of existing buildings. This factor is particularly important in historic villages, towns and conservation areas, where the cumulative loss of B&B bedstock could not in practice be replaced by new hotel accommodation.

No one could tell at that stage how serious a threat the bed tax actually was. However if the B&B sector had not put up a good fight using its most persuasive arguments at that stage, the idea may well have gathered momentum until it was unstoppable. Despite our arguments to Sir Michael, the bed tax was indeed included in the final Lyons Inquiry report as one of a number of possible means of raising money in future by local authorities.

Like most people, we don't usually celebrate on budget day, and that particular one (21 March 2007) started badly. After over a year, the final report was published – and it recommended that the government consider a new bed tax or local accommodation tax on B&Bs and hotels.

Just a few hours later, however, there was an emphatic response from Local Government Minister, Phil Woolas, at the Department for Communities and Local government, stating: 'We are not … inclined to focus on this area. The government does not intend to introduce a tourism tax.'

Looking back, the B&B sector can be proud of itself, as this is possibly the first instance where we have spoken with a combined voice and been heard by government. It was not the last!

The horrendous financial implications of the UK's budget deficit, however, have meant that the Lib-Con Coalition government is taking a very hard look at all areas of spend and all potential new areas of revenue. As part of that process, in the summer of 2010 a new Local Government Finance Act was being planned. So the BBA and the rest of the accommodation industry may well need to dust off their arguments against a bed tax and prepare for another battle.

The BBA will be keeping its members informed about the progress of any new bed tax proposal, should one arise.

PART TWO
RUNNING YOUR B&B

13
ORGANISING GUEST BEDROOMS AND CATERING

Designing guest bedrooms

Right at the beginning of this book we mentioned people's rising expectations and the fact that no amount of fancy décor or character will make up for having to leave your room and go down the corridor to have a pee. The fact is that almost everybody now expects to have at least a shower room and WC en suite wherever they stay.

If because of the layout of your property you are hoping to get away with one or more rooms having use of a separate bathroom, we would strongly caution against it. If you can think of another way round the problem which will give you an en-suite shower or bath, then do that instead. You would find that a room without an en-suite bath or shower will be very difficult to fill and that you could not charge anything like as much for it.

BATHROOMS

So our first point is: go for en-suite bathrooms every time. And if you are designing your bathrooms, use good-quality fittings, preferably in white rather than dark colours, and put in a tiled floor rather than a carpet (more hygienic, preferred by the official star-rating inspectors and easier to keep clean).

Ideally put in a bath *and* a shower – for example, shower doors above the bath and a shower fitment as well as taps. Many people prefer taking a shower and it saves your energy bills! The perfect arrangement is a bath *and* a separate shower cubicle, but this takes up much more space and costs more to install.

Bathrooms need pedal bins with removable linings and, for extra hygiene and ease of cleaning, line them with disposable bin liners and provide sanitary disposal bags.

You will need to ensure that guests have plenty of hot water for baths or showers at all reasonable times – so consider putting in a dedicated hot water tank for each guest room, with timed immersion heaters. Standard home hot-water systems with a single tank for all the guest rooms and your own family use probably won't be sufficient.

TOILETRIES

You must supply soap – a fresh soap for each guest – but, unless you are only going for the budget end of the market and a low star rating, you should also supply shampoo and bath foam, and perhaps conditioner, tissues, cotton wool, etc. At the top end of the market, a wide range of high-quality toiletries will be expected.

I always leave a new, wrapped, large bar of soap in the bathrooms but also leave an opened, hardly used bar of soap for guests' use as this is both economically and ecologically more sustainable. The guest who is squeamish can open the new soap or the guest who doesn't like waste will use the opened one.

BEDROOMS

Do think carefully when you are planning the layout, décor and fittings for your guest bedrooms. You may be 'stuck' with some things – room size and shape, ceiling height, view, etc. – which you cannot do much about, but almost everything else can be altered or enhanced. There is a great deal of difference to your guests between a thoughtfully planned room and one that has not been thought about. It is not necessarily expensive to get things right, and your guests will appreciate 'room planning' more than the niceties of décor, which may cost far more.

Standardise sheets and duvet covers so that linen is interchangeable and you never run out of linen on one-day changeovers. This also applies to towels.

As with getting into the shoes of your prospective customers to plan your marketing, so here you need to be a customer – stay in each room for a night. Sit and watch TV, make a drink, shave, have a bath, write a letter, do all the things that your guests will typically do. You will certainly notice things that did not occur to you before:

☐ Is there a shelf next to the mirror for toiletries or a shaving kit?

☐ Is the mirror at the right height and angle?

☐ Is the lighting right for shaving or applying makeup?

☐ Can you reach the bath towels from the bath?

☐ Where can you sit to write a letter?

☐ Can you control enough of the room's lighting without getting out of bed?

☐ Is there good bedside lighting each side of the bed for reading?

The list is endless – but think practically, in these terms. We are not talking about décor here, but the user-friendliness of your rooms.

Local information is very useful to guests and contributes to the official star-rating assessment. Collect leaflets and brochures from your local tourist office and from local attractions, and make them available to guests.

Always offer as much local information to guests as required. Being up to date on local restaurant opening times and taxi phone numbers/or train timetables can be invaluable to guests from far afield.

We find that the *Sherborne Shopping Guide* produced by the local Chamber of Trade and tourist office is excellent. It has a simple map of the town and details of all the shops, cafes, restaurants, etc., as well as attractions like the Abbey, museum and the two castles. We put one in each room, along with leaflets on local walks and other attractions nearby and within easy reach for a day out – for example, Bath, Stonehenge, the Jurassic Coast, Salisbury, the Fleet Air Arm Museum, etc. Think this through carefully. You may want to use a folder or ring binder in each guest bedroom, with leaflets and also with your own local recommendations for eating out, perhaps.

TEA AND COFFEE TRAYS

This is another feature that increases your assessment under the star-rating scheme, which will take into account its quality and range. Indeed, if you do not provide a tray, you must offer a hot drinks service morning and evening. We recommend putting a tray in every room, containing the following:

☐ a kettle;

☐ cups or mugs;

☐ tea, coffee and sugar in sealed packs or lidded containers;

☐ spoons;

☐ a small dish for used teabags; and

☐ biscuits and/or chocolates in sealed packs.

The kettle must not be on the floor of the bedroom, and we recommend it is a modern plastic kettle – safer and less liable to burn your guests' fingers.

Always have available small thermos flasks for supplying fresh milk for guests to use in their rooms where they can have their own tea or coffee. I always check whether guests require milk and offer to refresh it if they are staying more than one night. Don't use long-life milk (horrible!) and don't automatically put milk on trays without asking, as many people won't use it and you will waste milk.

Other equipment we recommend includes a hairdryer (these are very inexpensive now) and a TV. At The Pheasants, we have colour TVs with integral video players in each bedroom.

If your guest room televisions have a video/DVD option, it is a good idea to have some videos/DVDs on offer for guests to choose to watch if they find themselves stuck in their rooms for whatever reason or simply to keep young children amused. We have some videos available in a bookcase in the corridor outside the rooms and they have been much appreciated. (See page 55 on 'DVD Concierge Licence'.)

Serving breakfast

We have spent a huge amount of time on the 'bed' side of B&B. Luckily the second part of the duo is much more straightforward, if no less important.

Virtually every guest you have will take breakfast and most look forward to it as the highspot of staying in a family B&B. Your rooms or public facilities may not match up to a hotel, but your breakfast can easily beat the low-quality ingredients and tired buffet offered by most hotel chains. This is your chance to shine! A good breakfast will make up for imperfections in other areas and mean that your guests come back again and recommend you to their friends.

Breakfast is, with room changeovers, one of the two major areas of workload you will have as a B&B owner. You will spend many hours cooking, serving and clearing away breakfasts, so you need to get into a well planned routine.

HOURS

Firstly, some basic practicalities. It is essential that you make clear to your guests what the rules are on key things like check-out times and, of course, breakfast times. If this is vague or unclear, you will find guests coming down while you are still in bed or (more likely) you will still be waiting in the kitchen looking at your watch at the time you promised you'd meet your friend in town for coffee.

 Spell out breakfast times to each guest on arrival and clearly print it in room information sheets.

In our own B&B, our breakfast times are: 07.30 to 08.30 midweek and 08.30 to 09.30 on Saturdays and Sundays. This seems to work well, although sometimes after 55 minutes of waiting, we start to wish we had set a 30-minute range instead of an hour!

We have three rooms, but prefer not to have six guests all coming down for breakfast at the same time. So when we are full, and if the guests are happy to do so, we try to arrange more specific times with each couple to stagger their breakfast times.

INGREDIENTS AND MENU

Ingredients

Very clear and simple advice here: in our experience, it pays *not* to economise on ingredients! It is very easy to save a few pence with an inferior sausage or cheap bread, but customers will notice. We buy bread for around £2 a loaf because it is the best we can find, and we get lots of appreciative comments about it.

We have tried many different kinds of sausages and have settled at present on Westaways' premium West Country farmhouse sausages, which have an old-fashioned taste which has some of our guests waxing lyrical. One lady said that she had never tasted sausages as good as ours for 30 years! We could pay a quarter of the price to buy economy catering sausages, but our visitors would not go away so happy nor be as likely to come back or to recommend us to their friends.

When it comes to serving breakfast you should grill all bacon and cook eggs freshly to order, but a grilled sausage takes too long to cook so can be prepared slightly in advance and kept warm in a low oven.

Sign the 'pledge'

Alastair Sawday, the publishers of the *Special Places to Stay* series of guidebooks to British B&Bs, understand the importance of the quality of breakfast to B&B clients and have launched a 'Fine Breakfast Scheme' for the B&Bs they recommend. It is worth including the 'pledge' they ask B&B owners to sign.

FINE BREAKFAST SCHEME PLEDGE

1. I promise always to serve breakfasts of only the best available ingredients – whether organic or locally sourced.

2. Any certified organic ingredients will be named as such. (Note that the word 'organic' is a legal term. Any uncertified 'organic' ingredients cannot be described as organic.) Where there is a choice of organic certifier I will prefer the Soil Association if possible, recognizing that their standards are generally the most demanding.

3. All other ingredients will be, wherever reasonably possible, sourced locally from people/institutions that I know personally or have good reason to believe only provide food of the best quality.

4. Where I have grown food myself I will say so.

5. I will do my best to avoid shopping in supermarkets if good alternatives exist within a reasonable distance.

6. I will display the Fine Breakfast cards in the breakfast room or, if I prefer, in the bedrooms. (We accept that some of you may not want to use the cards.)

7. I know that the scheme is an imperfect instrument but accept its principles.

This gives you a good idea of the importance attached by this highly respected guidebook publisher to quality, local sourcing and the use of organic food as part of the overall customer experience in B&Bs.

Menu

Our typical breakfast menu at The Pheasants is as follows:

- ☐ Fresh orange or grapefruit juice.

- ☐ Freshly ground coffee (cafetière), English Breakfast tea or Earl Grey tea.

- ☐ Freshly made, wholemeal multigrain toast or farmhouse white toast.

- ☐ A selection of good-quality jams, honey or Frank Cooper's Oxford marmalade.

- ☐ Best English unsalted butter.

- ☐ A selection of cereals or muesli.

For those who like a cooked breakfast, our 'Full English Breakfast' is as follows:

- ☐ Grilled 'Westaways' award-winning West Country traditional pork sausage.

- ☐ Dry-cured grilled bacon.

- ☐ Fried free-range egg.

- ☐ Grilled fresh tomato.

Instead of a cooked breakfast we also offer a mixed-fruit compote with natural yoghurt and honey.

We offer a limited menu for breakfast but this does not stop most guests customising their breakfasts to suit – scrambled or poached or boiled eggs; baked beans on toast; even Coca Cola and soy sauce (separately!) are all breakfast requests we've had in the last year. The tip is be prepared. Take a deep breath and prepare each dish to the best of your ability. A guest would rather you supplied what they wanted rather than a blank refusal to try. You will also need to stock the whole range of breakfast beverages – coffee normal and decaffeinated, tea normal, herbal and decaffeinated.

All the above is included in the room price. Our only extra is Buck's Fizz (sparkling wine and orange juice) at £3.50 – though now we are licensed we would be happy to serve a bottle of champagne (or a round of scotch and sodas, come to that!) at breakfast, which would add to our revenue nicely.

SERVING, SEATING AND TABLE LAYOUTS

This is something which will be dictated as much by your dining-room space and furniture as by your or your guests' preferences. The temptation is to be like a hotel and to lay out separate tables for two and four, so guests can breakfast separately. This is indeed the safe option in many ways, but you have to have the room and the separate tables.

At our own B&B, we only have three letting rooms, so there is a maximum of six guests. Although our dining room has the space (under the previous owners, it was Sherborne's best restaurant), we have opted to lay six places around our dining table (which easily seats 10-12). When laid with silver candlesticks and a linen tablecloth, it looks festive and attractive, and we have had many comments of appreciation from guests about the conviviality of this idea.

We have discovered that a jug of iced water on the breakfast table is greatly appreciated, especially if the guest has had a heavy night of it the previous evening. This also saves you some costs as guests may drink less fruit juice, coffee or tea!

In our case, guests can keep themselves to themselves because there is enough space round the table, and they can opt to read a paper if they prefer not to speak to the other guests, but most do at least share a few words and some almost seem to be striking up new friendships over the bacon and eggs. That's when we feel that we have made the most of things and have maximised the advantages of a family B&B over any impersonal hotel.

Make sure you supply a daily newspaper for guests to enjoy before, during or after their breakfast. Also have a good range of reading material or magazines in the sitting room for guests to relax with (including local guide books).

Serving breakfast in bed

If you are concerned that you may lose out on guests wanting maximum privacy (perhaps romantic young couples?), then even if you have a large shared table like us, you could always offer a breakfast-in-bed option. People are prepared to pay extra for this service, and you could adapt your menu to avoid time-critical items like poached eggs. Options such as Buck's Fizz (if you have a licence) give you more revenue-earning opportunities and you may ease the pressure on your breakfast room this way.

Breakfast in bed requires the appropriate equipment: a trolley, perhaps, and bed trays – and don't stint on the napkins! Towelling robes are worth considering too if you are offering breakfast in bed. Breakfast in bed also introduces the risk of spillage of coffee or orange juice on bedding or carpets. The ideal layout is (if bedroom space permits) a table for two with two chairs in the bedroom itself.

When serving coffee in a cafetière, we always push the plunger down in the kitchen before taking it to the guests. A small thing to remember, but it saves the occasional explosion of coffee over your tablecloth as a clumsy guest pushes too hard or too fast! It's often the small tips which are most worth while.

Offering meals and drinks

If you are worried about the stresses and strains of running a B&B, relax – they are nothing compared with the stresses and strains of running a restaurant! It never ceases to amaze us how many people imagine that a love of food and wine qualifies them to open a restaurant. They seem to think that this is a self-indulgent and sybaritic lifestyle and ideal for a relaxed semi-retirement to escape the rat race of the office and the daily tube.

Nothing could be further from the truth. Restaurants are very hard work, hot, stressful and deprive you of any private life during the hours when everyone else is relaxing and socialising. Nobody but a madman would want to run one – unless they were absolutely obsessed and passionate about it and have never wanted to do anything else.

So, please, pause if you were considering serving meals as an extra. Unless you have worked in catering before, you are underestimating the work, the time commitment and the difficulty of making meals pay. Where it does work, it is either as a completely separate standalone business in its own right *or* in a strictly limited way – for example, a simple table d'hôte menu on Friday and Saturday nights only, offered at a B&B where guests have few alternative choices for meals nearby.

Having warned you off becoming a restaurateur, there are other, less all-consuming steps you could take as far as food is concerned to increase your revenue. We list a few below.

À LA CARTE BREAKFAST DISHES

You should include a standard English cooked breakfast or a 'substantial' continental breakfast in your room price. Over and above this, however, you could offer extra dishes priced individually, such as porridge, kippers, eggs Benedict, omelette Arnold Bennett or kedgeree. If you are licensed, you could offer Buck's Fizz or champagne (as we do at The Pheasants) – it won't sell every day but, when it does, it is extra revenue and all adds up.

Make sure that your appearance at breakfast is particularly scrupulous. Clean and tidy is a must for serving breakfast, whereas unkempt/ unshaven/slovenly gives all the wrong signals.

A word of caution: if you do decide to offer à la carte dishes, you need to keep the appropriate stock and, unless the dishes sell often, constantly buying some of the fresh ingredients (like smoked haddock) or making components like hollandaise sauce for eggs Benedict may not be worth it. You also need to price them at a level where the effort, ingredients costs and wastage are worthwhile and you are actually making a good gross profit.

PACKED PICNIC LUNCHES

Another idea to consider is offering packed picnics to your guests in summer, on a pre-ordered basis. You need to think through exactly what you would offer, produce a 'picnic box menu' or perhaps two or three alternatives, and set a price per person and a minimum number of people.

Again, the problem is stock. Ideally your options will be based on a combination of ingredients you carry in stock anyway (bread, eggs, drinks, etc.), packaged items that do not perish and fresh ingredients that are available every day at shops within a few minutes of your B&B. Otherwise you may think you have scored a big hit getting an order for lobster salad for £25, then find you cannot buy a lobster anywhere that day!

It is the practicalities, as ever, that you need to think through. These include the equipment. If you offer picnic boxes, you will need several suitable re-useable picnic sets, with a means of keeping drinks and fresh food cool.

MORNING COFFEE AND AFTERNOON TEA

There are meals that do not require much cooking but which could bring in extra revenue. Morning coffee with biscuits, cakes or pastries is one. When you look at the prices people are used to paying for a coffee and a pastry at Starbucks or Costa Coffee, for instance, it is easy to see how a few morning coffees can add up to a significant amount of extra revenue.

ALARM BELL

Don't cut corners on things your typical guest regards as important and/or are highly visible. Bulk-buying of loo paper is sensible, but serving your guests instant coffee or cheap and nasty cakes and biscuits is a cut too far.

The other meal is afternoon tea, and this can be quite substantial. It's up to you to decide whether a simple cream tea is enough or whether you want to offer a full English afternoon tea with finger sandwiches, pastries and cakes. Top London hotels now charge over £20 a head for this. How much you will be able to charge depends on your clientele and your location and the level of the market at which you operate.

Both these suggestions depend on your having a suitable place to serve coffees and teas and one that guests will enjoy lingering in – for instance, a comfortable lounge with a view of the garden or a conservatory. Your breakfast room may not be suitable.

14
MAKING BOOKINGS

One absolute fundamental in running a hospitality business is the crucial importance of the efficiency of your booking process. This includes responding to inquiries, checking availability, accepting or rejecting bookings, offering alternatives, handling deposits and – last but certainly not least – recording your bookings fully and accurately.

All this may seem obvious – and most is basically common sense – but it is surprisingly easy to forget one vital thing, and the results can potentially be very serious in cost, inconvenience and customer goodwill. So it is worth going through each element of the booking process.

Taking inquiries

You need to be contactable every waking hour, every day. If someone wants to check availability and make a booking, they will do it at their own convenience and in their own time, and this may be in the evening, on Sunday morning or while you are relaxing on the beach on holiday. That is the business you are in.

The second thing to remember is that, in most cases, if an inquirer cannot get an answer from you first time, they will simply call your competitors. So one missed phone call can lose a booking. We've returned phone calls within ten or twenty minutes to find that the inquirer has since booked elsewhere.

We'd recommend either:

☐ setting up an automatic divert to your mobile whenever you are not at home –

and keeping the mobile on of course!; or

☐ using BT's 1571 service with their text warning option – this sends your mobile a text message as soon as a message is left on your home phone. You can thus return calls very swiftly when you are out.

Last-minute bookings happen rarely but have to be dealt with when they occur. If referred by a fellow hotelier/B&B owner, the chances are it would be a genuine booker looking for accommodation. If this is the case make sure this guest gives you their full name and address and ensure they pay the full amount for their stay on arrival as a matter of policy. If you get a late-night phone call from someone who sounds vaguely dubious you should have no compunction to declare your rooms full.

Inquiries can also come in by email (e.g. from your website) and, again people tend to assume that email is instantaneous. At home, it is vital that you check and respond to emails frequently throughout the day. When you are away from home, you should either:

☐ have an auto reply email message asking people to call you with urgent inquiries; or

☐ have messages forwarded to a portable device or mobile phone, if you have a high-tech lifestyle.

Bookings book

So far, we have only talked about taking inquiries. The heart of your bookings system is (as the name implies) a book. Your bookings book. This could be a spreadsheet from specialist hotel-booking software but, for smaller B&Bs, you will probably do what we do and use a book.

The benefit of this low-tech approach is that you can easily take the book with you and use it anywhere, any time. You do not have to have a computer or laptop turned on. Don't forget that you *will* have to take the book with you everywhere – on the train, on holiday, on days out – or you won't be able to deal with the inquiries that can come in at any time, any day. Any one call could potentially be worth hundreds of pounds to you.

Ensure your bookings book is maintained accurately with all deposits logged and all information on the booking clearly marked. If any problem arises that needs to be clarified, contact your guest immediately. Honesty is the best policy in all matters and you could be surprised by their understanding attitude.

We simply buy an A4-size, hardback, week-per view diary for each year. This has three days down each left-hand page and four days down each right-hand page. Sundays are given less space than other days, but this is OK because you'll get fewer bookings on Sundays. At the beginning of the year, we rule each page vertically with two parallel lines, dividing it (and hence each day) into three equal parts. This gives us a column for each of our three letting bedrooms, which we head with each room name (always in the same order to save confusion!).

If you follow this method you have a very cheap, easy and convenient way to handle and record your bookings. Each room has a space of about 2 in. x 2.5 in. per day, which is ample to record (using small but clear writing) all you need to record:

☐ The date the booking is made and the method (e.g. email, phone).

☐ The name of the customer.

☐ Their home number.

☐ Their home address.

☐ Their mobile number (so you can contact them on the arrival day).

- ☐ Any special requests you have agreed (e.g. room type or extra bed).

- ☐ The price you have agreed.

- ☐ The deposit amount and method you have agreed.

- ☐ Their approximate arrival time (if known).

We put this information in the arrival day, then clearly mark the subsequent days of each booking with the second name and day number – e.g. for day two of Mrs Smith's four-day booking, we write 'SMITH 2/4'. On the final day, we write the total booking value, the deposit paid and balance due.

Always ensure that, wherever possible, you record your guest's mobile phone number when they book. This is invaluable as it enables you to contact the guest on the day to pinpoint their arrival time depending on the actual travel/traffic situation, and can allow you to leave the house rather than wait unnecessarily all day for the arrival of a guest who may have booked months earlier without any particular knowledge of an arrival time. This makes for a far more sensible use of your time.

We also have a ring binder, divided into months, to keep the letters received from bookers with their deposits. As soon as we receive a deposit we mark its receipt and the day of receipt in the book, then file the letter in the ring binder in date order (then bank the deposit immediately!).

Computerised and online booking systems

In recent years, more and more software packages have become available for B&Bs, designed for small premises and at prices a small B&B can afford. These level the playing-field with hotels, even allowing online booking from your website and opening up the possibility of gaining business not just from overseas from non-English speaking countries who might not telephone you but also from the big online agencies like lastminute.com, Expedia.com and many others. This is a growing sales channel and now you can – if you want – benefit from it.

For further information, see the following websites:

☐ eviivo (www.eviivo.com): their 'Frontdesk' system is the market leader for B&Bs, guest houses and small independent hotels and can give users access to bookings from lastminute.com, Expedia, etc., but they charge commission on all online bookings made, including directly at your own website.

☐ Angelfish Software (www.angelfishsoftware.co.uk) is a smaller business focusing on the small B&B. It provides diary or bookings management systems and full online booking.

☐ Guestlink (www.guestlink.co.uk).

☐ MyUK (www.myuk.travel).

☐ Keep Me Booked (www.keepmebooked.com).

☐ Guestlist (www.guestlisthq.co.uk).

Managing bookings

Now you have a system for taking and recording bookings. That is the easy part. The more difficult skill, which you will develop with experience, is in managing your bookings. By this we mean converting your inquiries into the most profitable and least troublesome outcome in bookings terms.

This is simple to say, but the skills involved are at the core of the success of every hospitality business. Whole books, hotel management courses and years of experience are devoted to the art of managing bookings.

If you are new to this, you may be wondering what can be so complex about simply answering the phone then writing each booking in your book. As with most things in life, it is not that simple! And with some intelligence and commercial instinct, you can make a huge difference to the profitability you actually achieve, given the same inquiries, to what you would achieve with a robotic approach.

CASE STUDY: MANAGING BOOKINGS

The following is a page from your bookings book:

	Room 1	Room 2	Room 3
	Double	*Twin*	*Double*
Wednesday	Smith		
Thursday	Smith		Brown
Friday		Jones	Brown
Saturday			Brown
Sunday			

(Jones requested a twin room specifically, as they are two sisters.) Now, suppose the phone rings and it is an inquiry from Mr White – he and his teenage son would like a twin room for four nights from Thursday. The obvious or robotic answer would be 'no – I'm afraid we cannot do it'. This is one of the most frustrating situations in the business: being faced with turning down a higher-value booking (in this case, four nights) because a low-value existing booking is blocking it.

Here is where your skills in booking management come in. You need to be sharp and quick thinking. The last thing you will want to do is turn away White's four nights because of Jones's one night.

A ruthless option would be to take the White booking then 'bounce' the Jones booking – i.e. tell Jones you cannot now take her booking, giving a suitably plausible reason (and having, with luck, already booked her a twin room provisionally nearby). Many hoteliers would not think twice about doing this, and it is commercially justifiable on the face of it. However, that should always be an absolute last resort.

Think harder. Room 1 is large enough to fit an extra folding bed, so why not put in the extra bed on Friday, move the Jones booking to Room 1 and accept the White booking in Room 2? You will have to give Ms Jones an explanation and perhaps even a discount or an added extra to make up, but that way you keep the Jones booking *and* take the White booking.

You have to think this through and react within seconds while White is on the phone. There won't be another chance, as White will phone your competitors if you can't take his booking. The golden rules are:

• don't turn down an attractive booking without having carefully considered all your options; and

• buy time if needs be.

Buying time can simply mean accepting the booking, knowing that you need to check another booking. If your ideal plan is not possible, going back to the person who has just booked within a few minutes or hours with profuse apologies is better than not having given yourself the chance to adjust another booking. And you may well be successful.

The above example is probably the simplest and most basic imaginable, but it serves to illustrate the kind of challenge you will get almost weekly and the quick-witted and hard-headed commercial instincts you will need to develop. It often becomes much more complex and demanding, as anyone in the business will tell you.

The challenges, and the skills required to deal with them, are not unique to B&Bs – they are part of running any business. If you have business experience *before* starting your B&B, it will give you a very good head start.

ALARM BELL

 Don't accept provisional bookings – be clear that a booking is either confirmed (by a deposit) or may be booked by someone else. And inquiries are coming in every day!

The art of managing your bookings could, as we said, fill a book in itself. But you are an intelligent person and the skills you need are a mixture of innate commercial instinct, experience, common sense and creativity. To be honest, anyone who needs to read a book to train themselves to *think* like a businessperson should probably not run a business.

We highlight below areas for you to think about, which may help you get to grips with things more quickly and so make a success of your business.

Our advice would be in three parts:

- aims

- rules

- flexibility.

The important thing is always to keep in mind some simple *aims*. Obviously, maximising revenue is the overall aim and, within that, getting longer bookings is an aim (fewer changeovers, fewer arrivals and departures). Getting multiple occupancy will be an aim (i.e. selling rooms as doubles or even family rooms rather than as single occupancy).

After the aims, having a few *rules* for bookings will help. An example is 'no single-night bookings will be accepted on Friday or Saturday nights in peak periods'.

How rigid these rules are is up to you. This is where the much-needed *flexibility* comes in:

- You will find it very difficult to apply any rules unless they are *written down* somewhere clearly – for example, on your website and/or in your leaflet. At least then you can point to the rule and it will be clear that you have not just invented it. It will be seen to be fair and non-discriminatory.

- It is not in your interests, however, to make the rules *too* prominent (for instance, by including them in adverts or guidebook listings). During a very quiet time you may welcome a single Friday night booking, so you would not want to discourage such inquiries before they pick up the phone.

❑   You will want to be able to use your discretion in applying the rules as part of your bookings management discipline. In busy times, you can rigidly apply rules like two-night minimums while, in quiet times, you can waive them. They are your rules after all, so you can break them!

Payment – watch your bottom line!

All our efforts as B&B owners are directed at attracting, then satisfying, our customers. The vital end result is the money they pay us. But many B&B owners forget to think about payment as much as they do about other aspects of their operation. Don't lose money by failing to plan how you take money!

DEPOSITS

Most of us learn the hard way that we *must* charge a deposit. The first one we waive will be the first one that does not turn up. Nothing is more frustrating than a 'no show' when you have turned away other customers. And if you have no deposit, it is a total loss.

The lesson is: *always* charge a deposit on booking.

PAYMENT TYPES

Cheques are only now of much use to small businesses (like B&Bs), so they are rapidly disappearing and are hardly ever used by anyone under 30. Also, late bookings do not allow time for a deposit cheque to arrive by post (let alone clear), so you will be taking a risk or losing business if you do not have some form of credit-card payment system.

Banks like to extract maximum profits by making set-up charges and monthly management charges (of at least £20), plus hefty commission, for a credit-card merchant account, and you may have to pay equipment rental and other fees too – assuming they even want to accept your business at all. This all became disproportionate for a small B&B.

An easy alternative is PayPal, the global email payments system (see www.paypal.co.uk).

PayPal is part of eBay and is used in over 55 countries. It allows you to accept payments by credit or debit card from anyone with an email address and Internet connection. Costs are around 3.4% plus 20p per transaction for small-volume users, with no other charges. This is much the cheapest option for the small B&B.

SPELLING OUT YOUR PAYMENT CONDITIONS

Put yourself on a strong footing in case of future disputes by making clear your payment conditions:

☐ Spell out in detail on your website and brochures your deposit level (for example: '£25 per room or 20% of reservation value, whichever is the higher').

☐ Spell out that the deposit is non-refundable (or specify the conditions for a refund).

☐ State when final payment is due (e.g. on arrival or on departure).

☐ State what your prices include (e.g. breakfast, taxes) and what they exclude (e.g. parking, drinks, etc.).

☐ Very importantly, spell out a clear scale of cancellation charges. These will typically be based on different flat rates or percentages of the reservation value, depending on the number of days from arrival on which the cancellation is made.

Think these rules through very carefully. If they are clear and reasonable, you should be able to enforce them in practice; if they are unstated or vague, you will have no chance.

As an example, here are the cancellation terms we use at The Pheasants:

Reservations cannot be guaranteed without pre-payment or receipt of an agreed deposit. Deposits are non-refundable. Cancellations will be charged as follows:

•   within 14 days of arrival: 25% of reservation value (or first night cost, whichever is the higher);

- within 48 hours of arrival: 50% of reservation value (or first night cost, whichever is the higher);

- within 24 hours of arrival: 100% of reservation value.

(The excess of the cancellation charge payable as above, over any deposit paid, is payable on cancellation.) If you have a travel insurance policy, you may be able to reclaim these cancellation charges should your reason for cancellation fall within your insurer's allowed criteria.

15
MANAGING ARRIVALS AND DEPARTURES

A 'diary discipline' that must become second nature to you is planning for arrivals, breakfasts, departures and changeovers. Unless you are always at home 24 hours a day, 365 days a year and have nothing else to do – which is highly unlikely! – you will, like us and like most B&B owners, be juggling your B&B work with other work and possibly also with family demands. An essential part of this 'plate-spinning' act is managing your B&B diary so that it is workable and allows for the other things you do in your life.

At the beginning it is easy to forget that you have more work the *day after* each booking entry than the day it appears in the bookings book. If Mr Smith arrives on Wednesday, then you have a breakfast to serve on Thursday. And if it is a one-night booking, a check-out a bit later on Thursday morning and then (and you can't delay this if there is a Thursday arrival in that room) a room changeover.

ALARM BELL

Don't buy duvet covers with buttons rather than poppers – you'll see why when you have to change several beds in a hurry, every day. Think about the time everything takes. (While we're about it, don't buy just one pair of matching linen sets for a twin room, as you'll only want to change one bed after a single-occupancy booking.)

If Mr Smith is staying for two nights or more and you have no other arrivals or departures on Thursday, then you know you only have breakfast duty on Thursday and are more or less free (apart from any room servicing).

Dealing with arrivals

Bear in mind that arrivals, although they do not involve much if any work, can be a huge time commitment. You (or someone else who knows what to do) must be around, within earshot of the doorbell, during the whole time period it is allowed (or reasonably expected) for your guests to arrive. This could be all afternoon and all evening if you are not careful.

Our strong recommendations, from painful experience, are:

☐ try to pin down every guest to an approximate arrival time; and

☐ get their mobile phone numbers so that you can contact them on the day.

It helps if you know a little about their journey. For example, if you know they planned to leave London at 2 p.m., you can estimate an arrival time and allow for any road problems you may hear on the radio. And don't be afraid to call them if they are late – it's better than waiting and wondering.

It is so easy simply to take a booking, getting the address and charging a deposit very efficiently, but forgetting to arrange an arrival time. You could literally be waiting, if you are really unlucky, from lunchtime to midnight if you have no expected arrival time and no means to contact the guests. At such times, running your B&B begins to lose its glister!

 Always *charge a non-refundable deposit. No deposit, no booking. Once they have paid (say) £25, they are less likely not to turn up (though it's not infallible – we have had no-shows who had paid a deposit).*

Guests should always be aware of your cancellation terms too, as they may well (for instance) be liable to pay the first night – i.e. more than their deposit – if they don't turn up. You may think that there is no chance of getting anyone to honour this, but we have done so on a number of occasions when let down by guests. Be firm and reasonable.

Calling guests the day before they are due often helps. You can remind them about arrival arrangements, and they will have up-to-date information about their travel plans and estimated arrival time.

Another important point is to give them clear directions as to how to find your B&B. Either send a map and directions or make sure they are aware of your location page on your website and advise them that they may find it useful to print it and bring it with them.

All simple things, but they can make a very real difference to your quality of life. Lay clear ground rules and be proactive and you will spend less of your life listening for the doorbell!

The rules about simple housekeeping matters, such as arrival, breakfast and checkout times, must be clear and must be communicated to every guest.

We are not suggesting that you rigidly apply these rules blindly to every guest – of course not. But a couple of examples will illustrate the value of rules:

☐ You state that arrivals can be between 4 p.m. and 6 p.m. A guest is coming to a wedding and asks to arrive at 12.30 p.m. to change. If you can be around at 12.30 p.m. and the room will be ready, fine – agreeing an exact arrival time is the ideal. That does not make the rule irrelevant because, without it, people would arrive between 10.00 a.m. and midnight (or even later). This is no exaggeration. We've had arrivals at 10.00 a.m. and at after midnight!

☐ You state that breakfast is served between 8.30 a.m. and 9.30 a.m. You make a point of telling every guest this on arrival and pointing out their information sheet in their room, where the times are also clearly printed. No guest can thus come down at 8.00 a.m. and reasonably expect breakfast to be served immediately. Likewise, if a guest comes down at 10.00 a.m., they cannot expect breakfast at all.

What do you do when a guest oversleeps? You have discussed breakfast times with your guest, you should even have these printed on the information sheet in their room. However, the guest has a late night and oversleeps. As it gets to the end of breakfast time you should contact them in their room with a gentle reminder about breakfast. If as expected they say they will be down shortly it is only polite to wait for them to appear (no doubt apologising profusely) and serve them breakfast. There is also the possibility that they may decline breakfast all together. Whatever happens it is essential that you do awake your guests and that they are not left to sleep undisturbed till lunchtime.

Stipulating check-out times

Departure or check-out times must also be very clear so that you can plan your life. If you have not stated a time clearly enough, don't be surprised if your guest lingers in their room until lunchtime, making you miss your 11.30 a.m. dental appointment.

Our check-out time is 11.00 a.m. If we have a guest who is getting a train at 2 p.m., we may invite them to wait in the drawing room downstairs for a further hour or so after 11.00 a.m. as long as they have vacated the room by then so it can be stripped and cleaned (and as long as we do not have to go out ourselves at 11.00 a.m.).

Organising your other commitments

You must keep an eye on your bookings book to plan each week well ahead, bearing in mind the arrivals, departures, breakfasts and changeovers you have each day and how these fit with the rest of your commitments. This is also something to keep in mind as you decide to accept each booking.

If you have another diary or diaries (say, personal and business) in addition to your bookings book, you will need to consult them all as you take each booking, and on a daily basis as you keep all those plates spinning.

Arranging your own holidays

As we are on the subject of diary disciplines, this is a good place to mention holidays – your holidays. You may be, as we have always been (in our case, typical for travel industry people!), late bookers of holidays. We rarely booked our own holidays more than a few short weeks ahead. This has to change when you run a B&B. You have to fix your holiday *dates* (you can book the destination as late as you like) a long way in advance – before you start to get any bookings for that part of the year. This tends to mean at the beginning of the year or even well before Christmas the previous year in our case. And for many traditional seaside-resort B&Bs, it will mean at least a year ahead as many guests book their next year's summer break while on this year's.

Needless to say, if you don't decide your holiday dates and clearly block them off in your bookings book, you will take bookings scattered across every week of the season and be unable to go away at all. This does not only apply to longer holidays of a week or two but to weekends or long weekends or public holidays like Easter, which you want to keep for yourselves and your family. By definition these will book up soonest so, unless you want to be working all year, think ahead and block off *your* days in the bookings book!

ALARM BELL

Don't forget to plan your own holidays well ahead or you will find you can never get away. You are running a B&B to enhance your quality of life, not to erode it!

Again at the risk of stating the obvious, if you want an early start on your holiday day, it means blocking off the previous day too, or you may be tied to a breakfast, checkout and even a changeover on the first day of your holiday – not very useful if it is day one of a two-day break.

Again, thinking through all this will bring home to you – if you haven't realised already – just how much of a time commitment you will be taking on when you start your B&B. If you are starting to get second thoughts, thank us – the price of this book is nothing compared with what you would have spent starting a business and then closing it down later. And if you are not having second thoughts, good – you are well prepared, and planning ahead clearly holds no worries for you. Running a B&B should not do, either.

Keys

If you have not run a B&B or hotel before, you do need to think carefully about keys.

BEDROOM KEYS

You may think that you don't need lockable bedrooms. Forget it. When you go and stay in a hotel, do you leave your room unlocked? When you are browsing the local antique shops, are you happy to think of all your personal things being in an open room back at the B&B where you are staying? Most testing of all, do you enjoy taking a shower, or doing even more intimate things, in a house full of strangers with the door unlocked?

People want the reassurance of turning the key as they close the door behind them, both on the way in and on the way out. It is as simple as that. The only question is: what sort of key and what your key policy is ('hand in on going out', or 'keep with you during your stay'?).

FRONT-DOOR KEYS

Do you give your guests front-door keys? This is one of the ones that worried us most before we started (though not much since, which may either reassure you or convince you of our recklessness). Guests will want to come and go when they choose, within reason. Are you going to be there every minute of every day to let in a guest? This is not a trick question but it needs thinking about.

You may say 'I never go out anyway', but Sod's Law states that the one time you do leave the house for half an hour to buy eggs, orange juice and sausages will be the exact moment your guest returns from a long and tiring walk with an urgent need for a bath, a pee and a cup of tea. And believe us, they will not be in a happy mood by the time they have waited on your doorstep in the rain for 25 minutes.

And it is not just daytime but night-time too. You may be in, but you may well be in bed. Being woken up at 1.45 a.m. by the doorbell as your guests return from a wedding reception will not make you want to repeat the experience. So all in all, you will probably conclude (as we did) that you should give each guest two keys – their room key and a key to the front door.

If this idea fills you with horror, then it has been worth buying this book! At least it's better to confront the key issue now and work out how to address it than to come up against the problem by trial and error later. If the idea of giving strangers a key to your home is anathema to you, then you should probably reconsider the whole idea of running a B&B. Again, better to have got there for the price of a book than to have started a business before falling at the first post!

We have a lot of weekend guests who come down for weddings. In many ways these are not the most ideal guests. They rush in, in a hurry to change for their wedding, and then dash out for the ceremony and reception returning usually in the very early hours of the morning waking up the whole household as they crash up the stairs. One such guest, in a party of six, arrived back at 2 a.m. We became aware of someone going up and then down the stairs. Having realised that they hadn't left the house I set off in my dressing gown to investigate. I found this guest in the kitchen rummaging through a drawer with a bottle of our red wine under his arm – he was searching for a corkscrew. On being challenged he expressed surprise that we didn't have a bar or were licensed (regardless of the fact that he was helping himself) and then requested a flask of milk to have a coffee in his room. He certainly needed several black coffees as his state of undress attested to a certain degree of over-indulgence. He retired to his room and failed to turn up for breakfast the next morning, no doubt embarrassed by his late-night shenanigans.

There is not much more to add on front-door keys except that a high-tech (and expensive) alternative exists to the old-fashioned key: a push-button keypad. However, unless you change the combination every day, you are in a worse situation from a security point of view. Similarly, older, short-sighted or tipsy guests – and probably most others too – will forget the combination or enter the wrong one, so you will get that 1.45 a.m. doorbell and that angry guest waiting on your doorstep anyway.

Our experience has convinced us that the best policy is to give guests a set of two keys – bedroom and front door – to keep with them during their stay. It is vitally important, then, to:

☐ use good-sized, sturdy key rings with clearly labelled tabs;

☐ remember always to get the keys back in your hands as each guest checks out. Most will never remember that the keys are in their pocket until they are 85 miles up the motorway or, if they are flying abroad the next morning, as they rummage for euros in a Viennese coffee shop two days later; and

☐ make up at least three sets of keys for every room: one for the guest, one as your master set for checking and servicing the rooms, and one as a spare in case (it will happen occasionally, believe us) you forget to ask for the keys and a guest goes off with them.

You should also find a good local locksmith who can cut new keys at short notice and who can change your front-door lock if a set is lost completely or if you are worried that a key may have fallen into the wrong hands.

16
DEALING WITH DIFFICULT CUSTOMERS AND COMPLAINTS

Note: all the names in this chapter have been changed to preserve anonimity.

Tackling difficult customers

If you haven't sold services to the public before, you are in for some interesting experiences and a masterclass in human nature. You will realise that, however much care you take to make everything as near perfect as possible, there will be times when you get complaints. It is a fact of life in any service business.

The good news is that the vast majority of people (at least in our experience) are polite, understanding, well behaved and appreciative; in short, 'nice'. The bad news is that the very small minority who are not will give you your fair share of headaches.

To put this in context and to reassure you, in our first 400 paying customers from a standing start as B&B virgins, we had three problems and three unpleasant experiences. We learnt useful lessons from some, though others simply have to be put down to experience, part of the wear and tear of life. It may help you to hear about them because they must be fairly typical of what you may encounter.

THE ABSCONDER

This was our worst incident so far. A call came through one afternoon from the town's most expensive hotel, saying a Mr Baker had arrived to stay the night but they were full. Did we have a room free? We did. Mr Baker duly arrived by taxi five minutes later, saying that his car had broken down on his way back from Cornwall. He was fairly presentable, and polite and grateful to have found a room.

The next morning while we were serving breakfast to other guests we heard a noise which we later realised was our front door closing. Mr Baker had undone two bolts and slipped out by the exit he saw was unobserved. A quick check outside yielded no trace of Mr Baker, who was clearly nimbler than he looked.

His room held various debris, including a bag of assorted hotel soaps and shampoos, and the smell of cigarettes. The fact that he had been smoking in his room, oddly enough, angered us almost as much as the fact that he had left without paying. The smoking in our home felt somehow more personal a violation than his crime, which in effect was theft.

We immediately reported Mr Baker to the police and were agreeably surprised when they took DNA samples, and amazed when they found a match. We heard later that our former unwelcome guest had been arrested and our crime added to his long and impressive list of charges.

I always think that airing guest bedrooms really well between guests is so important. We open the door and windows, even in winter, for a good hour or so while we are cleaning and hoovering to freshen up the rooms really well. We're sure it is not just psychological but makes a real difference. A genuinely fresh, clean smell is so much better than the stale smells masked with air-freshener spray which you encounter in some places.

Lesson: this emphasises how important it is to keep security of payment in mind. Clearly, alarm bells should have rung because of the circumstances: arrival without notice, without a car and with little luggage (a backpack). We were probably unconsciously reassured by the fact that he was 'referred' by an expensive hotel, but of course the hotel knew no more about Mr Baker than we did (he had told them a different story, we discovered). We even failed to ask him for his home address and phone number.

Nothing you do short of taking full payment *on arrival* rather than departure will stop this happening, but our failure to take any details from him at least opened the possibility of an opportunistic, spur-of-the-moment departure. If we had taken his address and contact details on arrival, and if this was opportunistic rather than premeditated, we might have avoided it.

Having said that, such a habitual offender would be likely simply to give a false name and address, although one of the oddest things about our Mr Baker was that he did in fact give us his real name.

THE PARTY GIRLS

We had a two-night booking for a twin room from Miss d'Arcy who casually mentioned that they would be arriving late. David's big mistake was not to query exactly what 'late' meant. From her tone he assumed it simply meant the evening rather than the afternoon. Never assume! We did at least get her mobile number, so when it got to 9.00 p.m. and no one had arrived or phoned, David called Miss d'Arcy to check whether they needed directions to find us in Sherborne.

Miss d'Arcy breezily said that they had been a little held up leaving London and were just getting on to the M25 at that point. This meant they were at least two and a half hours away, perhaps more. When David said this, our guest asked 'is that a problem?' Of course, we said 'no'. No problem for her – just highly inconvenient and annoying for us!

A Mercedes sports car finally pulled up outside at about midnight, with much noisy door slamming, and David was greeted by two expensively educated and expensively dressed twenty-something women with the words 'I know we are a bit late but I guarantee I have had a *much* worse day than you have' boomed out loud enough to ensure even our deafest neighbour was woken up.

Our guests talked loudly all the way up two flights of stairs as David took them to their room and carried their bags – just in case any of our guests (or family) were not quite fully awake again.

Please try to be as welcoming as humanly possible when guests first arrive at your door. All good/bad impressions are created within the first few seconds of meeting someone, and it is imperative that you make your 'paying guest' feel that you are really pleased to have their company in your house. Whatever you are really thinking is best kept under wraps until you are in the privacy of your own rooms.

The following night Miss d'Arcy and friend went to a wedding reception, from which they returned at 2.30 a.m. the next morning, then spent the next hour and a half creeping up and down our (creaky) stairs and sitting in our courtyard smoking and talking with a young man. As our bedroom window is on the first floor above the courtyard, all this finally put paid to any sleep we had hoped for that night.

When Miss d'Arcy checked out (after coming down for breakfast at the very last possible moment), she told us that she had a problem with her car that needed fixing before she could drive back to London and asked which garages were open. There are certainly no Mercedes dealerships open in our part of rural Dorset on a Sunday morning, and David asked what sort of problem the car had. Our guest explained that she had parked the car on Friday morning in London with the roof down and it had rained, which had made the seats damp and made the car smell inside, which she could not possibly put up with for three hours. We sympathised deeply with her difficulties.

Lesson: always pin down expected arrival times and obtain a mobile number. Unfortunately, there is not much more you can do about selfish and inconsiderate guests. Luckily, most are not like that.

SPACED OUT AND SMELLY

This was our first negative impression of a guest, fairly soon after we started. So far, everyone had been fine and things had gone very smoothly. Today Louise opened the door to a guest from Chicago who had booked in for five days at fairly short notice without asking us any questions. Her first impression of Mr Kallman worried her so much that she momentarily considered not letting him in. He was scruffy, dishevelled and seemed to have trouble speaking – and he gave off a very strong and unattractive odour.

Louise took him to his room and called David (who was working elsewhere). We decided that, on balance, everything might be explained by his coming straight from a long flight and train journey. We would do nothing yet but keep a close eye on him and perhaps lock family bedroom doors.

Ensure all your own private rooms are marked as such with 'PRIVATE' signs above or on the door. This sounds obvious but it does help to mark out where the guests can or can't go and stops you coming across guests in unexpected places (and deprives them of the excuse that they did not realise the room was off limits).

In fact Mr Kallman presented a rather pathetic figure and, the following morning at breakfast, David was rather sorry for him as he blinked vacantly and struggled for words. He said he had jet-lag but it seemed more than that to us. When David asked him whether he preferred coffee or tea at breakfast, he managed at the second attempt to pronounce the word 'Coke'. We had to break the news that we had no Coca Cola in stock.

Lesson: there isn't one here really, except that things are usually nothing like as bad as you fear they might be. Mr Kallman worried us at first but in the event caused no problems.

Handling complaints

WRONG ROOM

We showed a married couple to their room – a double. They mentioned that they had requested our twin room. David apologised – we had missed this mention in their letter – and said that unfortunately it was not possible to move them as the other two rooms were full. He asked if this was OK and they said yes. It was not mentioned again during their two-day stay and, when they left, they thanked us for an enjoyable stay and wrote a positive comment in our visitors' book. A week later, we received an email from the couple asking for a substantial refund because they had not had the room they had wanted.

We dealt with this by replying to explain that we had apologised if we had missed their room request and that they had accepted this. At that point they could have left. They had also said their stay was enjoyable. So we wrote that they had received the service they had booked from us: two day's bed-and-breakfast accommodation. We did not feel that a refund was justified.

This couple, we later found out, then contacted our local tourist office to ask whether other complaints had been received about our B&B. The tourist office told them that they had only had good reports about The Pheasants.

After another indignant email from them criticising us for not agreeing to a refund, the couple gave up.

Lesson: 1) read booking letters carefully and note specific requests; 2) apologise and ask if it is OK (i.e. does the customer still want to stay) if something like that does happen; and 3) explain carefully, and stick to your guns, if you genuinely feel a refund is not justified.

MISSING FORK

Another, long-married couple seemed clearly not to be enjoying themselves. They were not chatty, they sat in silence and Mrs made a disparaging comment about the flowers in our drawing room. She said they were 'dead, dead, dead – very depressing'. As it happens they were a little faded, but it is a subjective judgement as to when fresh flowers no longer look attractive and should be binned. We were a little stung by this comment and immediately replaced all the flowers in our public rooms.

At breakfast, Mr had to ask for a fork as it had been missed from his table setting – the first and only time this has ever happened. They also seemed very surprised that their room had not been 'serviced' (i.e. the linen and towels changed) after their first night. We explained that, as a B&B rather than a hotel, we did not change linen daily.

During breakfast it always pays to check regularly whether guests require any more tea/coffee/toast, etc. Even though the answer may usually be no it reaps dividends in making the guests feel that they have been particularly well cared for and attended to and they leave with that lasting impression.

When they left, this somewhat sour-faced couple made no comment but, again a week or so later, they wrote us a letter saying that they felt we ran the B&B 'for your own convenience rather than for your guests'.

As we take huge pains to make our guests feel welcome, this comment really hurt. It is very hard not to take these things personally, and we did feel that personally. We gritted our teeth, though, and thought hard. We tried to be self-critical: perhaps we had had an off-day? Perhaps we should have changed those flowers a day earlier, not slipped up on our table settings and explained properly our room servicing policy rather than assume that everyone knew what to expect?

We wrote a long and, we think, fair letter back in response and redoubled our efforts to keep an eye on the smallest detail. We also set out our policy on changes of linen and towels (which are in accordance with the 2006 five-star B&B VisitBritain standards) in our room information sheets.

Always supply guests with a printed list of information on your B&B in their rooms (e.g. breakfast times, checkout times, payment details, etc.).

Lesson: this one shows that the most difficult complaints are not about any one thing but are a litany of minor things. What is the underlying cause? Perhaps the real reason they were unhappy had more to do with the weather or having had a marital row than with our B&B keeping. Even so, always make yourself see things through the customer's eye and – as in this case – there are usually positive lessons to learn which will help you in the future.

Responding to complaints

This very limited experience of difficult B&B customers, and a combined 30 years or so of experience dealing with difficult customers in other industries (including hotel and holiday customers), has taught us a few fundamental rules it is best to stick by:

- ☐ Listen sympathetically.

- ☐ Don't justify or be defensive.

- ☐ Buy time. Don't commit immediately to specific recompense.

- ☐ Analyse the complaint carefully and dispassionately, putting yourself in the customer's shoes.

- ☐ Get back to the customer as soon as you can and explain your response and your reasoning carefully. Rationally argued and quantified explanations carry most weight.

- ☐ Don't get angry or emotional.

- ☐ Try to avoid entering into a negotiation.

- ☐ Be polite and respectful – even if the customer is not!

- ☐ Try to learn from complaints and improve your service.

And to reassure those who have never dealt commercially with the public before: it is not as bad as you fear. As we have said before, the vast majority of people are like you: nice, polite and reasonable. A tiny minority are not.

17
MARKETING YOUR B&B

What is marketing and why do you need it?

There are a lot of misconceptions about marketing. Many of these are fostered, intentionally or otherwise, by marketing people. Because people with 'marketing' in their job title want to preserve an aura of mystique about their profession – and hence add to their own value – they tend to complicate what they do and obscure it with jargon. Paradoxically, this has actually devalued marketing in the eyes of the general public, who think of marketing as something only done by specialised departments in large companies.

Marketing is really just salesmanship. It is an absolutely essential part of running any business, whether it is labelled marketing or not. Think of it as all the things you have to do within your business to enable the sales to come in and the business to make a profit.

So marketing includes getting your décor right for your customers, setting your prices, how you greet and correspond with your guests, the quality of your breakfast ingredients and many other things, as well as the more obviously marketing areas of advertising and promotion.

Make sure the first impression is always favourable for every arrival – especially your own welcome. The first few minutes can set the tone for your guest's whole stay. Set the scene with lighting, a log fire, flowers and some well placed glossy magazines – and perhaps offer tea and biscuits or a cold drink on the house?

Anything that makes your guests more likely to come back is marketing. Everything that persuades your guests to pay a little bit more, or stay a little bit longer, is marketing. And anything that makes the phone ring is marketing.

Positioning and target audience

By now you have looked at the location of your B&B and the property itself and its character, size, setting, décor and facilities, and you have decided on your target market(s). This might include, say, families on a budget wanting to be near the seafront of the resort or couples aged 30 and older staying for cultural short breaks or foodies staying nearby a renowned restaurant. There is no limit to who your target audiences are nor where they come from, and they will be different for every reader of this book. The point is, you have thought all this through and you have identified your own market.

The next thing is to think yourself into the shoes of each audience type you have identified. If they were coming to your area, how might they decide where to stay and what factors would make them decide to stay with you? This should give you a few possible leads to pursue.

Just to give two specific examples: if your B&B overlooks a surfing beach in Cornwall and your market includes surfers, then surfing magazines, local surf shops, surfing associations and clubs, and surfing websites would all be worth looking at for collaboration or advertising. Alternatively if your market includes genteel older ladies seeking country weekends, perhaps a small ad in *The Lady* may work well.

The examples themselves are not important, and are probably not relevant to you. The essential thing is to:

☐ identify your target audience; and

☐ get into their shoes and try to shadow their thought processes to identify the areas you can reach them.

Networking and local contacts

Inevitably you will be thinking a lot about advertising your B&B nationally and internationally, but don't forget that local contacts can be just as important. And often these don't cost anything.

Network locally with those who run attractions, wedding venues, the tourist office, restaurants – even other hotels and B&Bs – and make sure they know about your B&B and why they should recommend you to visitors.

Sit down and think through all the reasons people come to stay in your area, what they do when they get there and even where else they come to stay apart from your B&B. Even competitors may be able to help you!

Taking the example of our own B&B. People come to Sherborne for weddings at the Abbey or the Castle, for functions at the various boarding schools here and to explore and admire the historic architecture. We therefore contacted the Castle so that couples planning to marry there included The Pheasants on their list of local accommodation for wedding guests; we did the same with the Abbey. We contacted the schools and got put on the information they send to parents and on their websites. We made sure we were listed on the official town website. And we established friendly relationships with the hotels in town and with the other B&Bs.

We now get bookings referred by the hotels or other B&Bs when they are full and, in return when we are full, we refer inquirers to the hotels or B&Bs who have done the same for us. That is the best kind of marketing: simple, effective, permanent and costs nothing!

Exactly whom you will benefit from contacting will vary in each location, so think though the equivalents in your own location. If people come to visit a particular attraction, see if you can be added as a link on the attraction's website for those who want to find local accommodation. Go in and speak to the people running the attraction and, crucially, to those who deal with clients on the phone. Tell them about your B&B and why they should mention it to anyone who asks where they could stay nearby. Leave copies of your leaflet, flyer or cards to remind them.

It is good to build up relationships with local restaurants and hotels for mutual promotion. It is useful to be able to provide a top-up service for hotels who may have overbooked and to help them out of a tight spot. In the same vein, restaurants may need to book or offer recommendations for accommodation to large parties who need to come from afar for an event. Nearby hotels can help you as well as being competitors – and you can help them in return by referring inquiries when you are full.

Call and speak to your competitors and suggest co-operation. We visited the nearest B&B to us and invited the owner to visit The Pheasants, and we have since helped each other by referring potential guests when we are full. This benefits us both, and a further incidental benefit comes from talking to other B&B owners about common problems and challenges. You can often learn very useful things.

Marketing nationally and internationally

THE 'OFFICIAL' STAR-RATING SCHEME

The 'official' classification scheme for B&Bs in the UK is based on inspections by Quality in Tourism or by the AA, whose ratings are recognised by all the UK's tourism authorities (VisitBritain, VisitScotland and the Wales Tourist Board).

The previous 'diamond' rating scheme for B&Bs and guest houses was replaced in 2006 by a new classification scheme based on stars. B&Bs are rated from one to five stars according to detailed criteria agreed by the two inspecting bodies and the tourism authorities.

The new star-rating scheme is described in detail in the 36-page booklet, *Common Standards for Guest Accommodation*, published jointly by the Wales Tourist Board, VisitBritain, VisitScotland, RAC Motoring Services and the AA in 2005 (the RAC has since stopped inspecting hotels and B&Bs so is no longer involved).

The 'Common Standards' define a B&B as 'accommodation provided in a private house, run by the owner and with no more than six paying guests'. If your establishment can accommodate more than six paying guests, it would be defined as a 'Guest house', whose full definition is:

> *Accommodation provided for more than six paying guests and run on a more commercial basis than a B&B. Usually more services, for example dinner, provided by staff as well as the owner.*

For further information, go to www.qualityintourism.com

Minimum requirements

The key minimum requirements under the star-rating scheme at one-star level are as follows:

☐ A cooked breakfast or substantial continental available.

☐ Proprietor and/or staff available for guests' arrival, departure and at all meal times.

☐ Once registered, resident guests have access to the establishment at all times unless previously notified.

☐ All areas of operation meet the minimum quality requirements for cleanliness, maintenance and hospitality as well as facilities and the delivery of services.

☐ A dining room or similar eating area available unless meals are only served in bedrooms.

☐ You must meet all the current statutory obligations and provide public liability insurance cover.

Key requirements at each rating level

As well as enhanced quality standards at each higher star rating, there are certain key requirements you will need to achieve:

Three star and above

☐ Access to both sides of all beds for double occupancy.

☐ Bathrooms/shower rooms cannot be shared with the proprietor.

☐ (From 1 January 2008) a washbasin in every guest bedroom (either in the bedrooms or en-suite/private facility).

Four star

☐ 50% of guest bedrooms to be en-suite or with private facilities (from 1 January 2008).

Five star

☐ All guest bedrooms to be en-suite or with private facilities (from 1 January 2008).

There are five levels of quality rating, from one to five stars. To obtain a higher star rating you will need to provide enhanced quality standards across all areas, with particular emphasis in five key areas:

☐ cleanliness

☐ hospitality

☐ breakfast

☐ bedrooms

☐ bathrooms.

Cleanliness is given great emphasis in the common standards, which state:

cleanliness is of paramount importance to guests in every type of establishment so a high standard of cleanliness must be achieved and maintained throughout the property:

• *Bathrooms and shower rooms should be clean and smell fresh with particular attention paid to fittings and sanitary ware, plug-holes, shower curtains, flooring, mirrors, extractor fans and towels.*

• *You will also need to pay special attention to wherever guests have direct contact – seating, crockery, cutlery, glassware, beds, bedding and linen.*

• *All bedrooms and bathrooms should be cleaned and checked daily to ensure a very high standard of cleanliness.*

We have not the space here to reproduce all the detailed criteria in the common standards document. Much of it is basic common sense and fairly obvious – for example, the requirement for the proprietor or staff to be on duty during arrival and departure periods and at meal times, and the requirement to describe your amenities and facilities fairly to all inquirers.

Much detail is devoted to the spaciousness of rooms and adequacy of lighting, heating and ventilation, but here you can be guided by your own standards and expectations when you stay in a B&B or hotel.

Ensure all public areas, such as guests' sitting room/dining room, are clean, tidy and welcoming, with fresh flowers or pot-pourri to provide an inviting scent.

We mention a few of the less obvious or more specific requirements as this may be helpful.

Bedroom sizes

Bedrooms smaller than the following sizes are unlikely to meet the minimum requirements:

Single room:	5.6 m²	60 ft²
Double room:	8.4 m²	90 ft²
Twin room:	10.2 m²	110 ft²

For two to five star ratings, rooms would be expected to exceed considerably the above minimum sizes. Ceiling heights must be sufficient for a person of 6 ft to move around without stooping.

Minimum bed sizes and bed specifications

Single bed:	190 × 90 cm	6 ft 3 in × 3 ft
Double bed:	190 × 137 cm	6 ft 3 in × 4 ft 6 in

Beds of 183 × 75 cm/6 ft × 2 ft 6 in are only acceptable for children and can only be used as part of a family room. Beds of 190 × 122 cm/6 ft 3 in × 4 ft will be acceptable for single occupancy only. Rooms with bunk beds only are not acceptable for adult use. Bunk beds must have at least 75 cm/2 ft 6 in clear space between the mattress of the bottom bed and the underside of the top bed.

All mattresses should be comfortable and have mattress protectors and a sprung interior or be made of foam or similar. Plastic or rubber mattress protectors are not acceptable except for small children. All beds and mattresses should be of sound condition with a secure headboard or equivalent. The use of pillow protectors is recommended as best practice. One hundred per cent artificial-fibre sheets are not acceptable.

Changing the beds

All beds should be made daily. There should be two pillows per person, with a non-allergenic alternative offered to feather pillows or duvets.

All bed linen should be fresh for each new guest. It should then be changed once every four days, except where there is a clearly advertised environmental policy that invites guests to agree to less frequent linen changes (e.g. weekly).

Buy the widest ironing board available – it cuts down on ironing time. Sheets have to be shuffled fewer times on a larger board.

Other things you will need to provide include:

☐ Either a morning and evening hot-drinks service or a tea/coffee tray in the rooms.

☐ Printed advice displayed in the bedrooms on how to obtain emergency assistance at night.

☐ An iron and ironing board available to guests on request and advertised in the bedrooms.

☐ Fresh soap for each new letting.

☐ Hot water at 'all reasonable times'.

☐ In bathrooms, a lidded bin or an open bin with sanitary disposal bags provided.

☐ A clean hand and bath towel for each guest, which (unless there is a clearly advertised environmental policy) should be changed at least every three days.

☐ A clean bath mat for each new let.

'Accessories'

The common standards refer to some facilities and accessories that are not requirements but which may be provided in the bedrooms and which, if provided, will contribute to the level of the quality assessment. These include ingredients and equipment for making hot drinks, colour TV, telephone, fresh fruit, flowers, radio, hairdryer, sweets, mineral water, reading material, clothes brushes, mending kits, biscuits, trouser press, fridge, writing materials, tissues and hot-water bottles. If extra items such as these are provided, the document states: 'their quality, range, presentation and ease of use will all be taken into account in the quality assessment'.

The new star-rating scheme will, like the previous diamonds scheme, become well recognised and trusted by the public. The fact that a B&B has been independently inspected and assessed to official criteria is a great reassurance to potential guests and gives the B&B valuable credibility. This is worth a lot to you in marketing terms: just saying you have been officially rated at say three star or four star says more as far as a guest is concerned than pages of copy you have written yourself in your brochure or on your website.

ALARM BELL

Don't tell your guests how hard you are working or how difficult your day has been – they are paying to relax and enjoy themselves away from domestic tedium, and feeling that they are adding to your burden won't help.

Unless you intend to run your B&B on a very small scale or occasional basis only, we would recommend that you apply for an official star rating. This is because of the credibility factor just touched on, and also because this allows you to benefit from the tourism promotion budget of your local tourist authority. Now it is becoming usual for tourist authorities to list and promote only B&Bs which have been officially star rated (our own West Dorset happens to be one). This means that, if you are not officially rated, you miss out on this promotional opportunity.

Before going ahead, however, we recommend that you send for the full information pack from Quality in Tourism, including the *Common Standards for Guest Accommodation* booklet, and study it in detail. Then decide what star level you would like to achieve, bearing in mind your prices, your target market and your competitors.

The common standards criteria will give you a good idea of what star rating you might achieve as things are. You might want to do some work to ensure that, by the time the inspector calls, you have a chance of achieving the rating you want – assuming this is higher.

For example, we postponed our own inspection to upgrade a couple of bathrooms. We'd rather wait and hope to get a higher rating than have had an early inspection and, in all probability, get a lower official rating than we would like.

For further information, including latest fees and details about the assessment process, or to apply for a star rating under the new scheme, go to www.qualityintourism.com, call 0845 300 6996 or write to: Quality in Tourism, Farncombe House, Broadway, Worcester, WR12 7LJ.

ADVERTISING IN NEWSPAPERS AND MAGAZINES

If the 'putting yourself in your customers' shoes' exercise leads you to consider advertising in a newspaper or magazine:

- ☐ keep the advert small to save money;

- ☐ do a short test run first to gauge response before committing to weeks or months;

- ☐ think about seasons and timing: save your money for key booking times; and

- ☐ be careful about the section you go in: is 'short breaks' or 'luxury breaks' better than 'Lake District', for instance?

For lineage adverts – the small classified ads consisting of words only, without graphics or frames – the first word or two is vital. This will be printed in bold and needs to attract the eye of your perfect prospective guest. Think this through, with a copy of the publication in front of you. If you are going in under 'Cornwall', don't make 'Cornwall' your first word – they know that already! Make your town or village your first word (e.g. 'St Mawes'), or make one of your unique selling points your first words (e.g. 'Sea Views'). If you are going to be listed under a non-geographical heading like 'UK Short Breaks', then name your location in your first word.

Make your advert full of information but concise, and with a telephone number and, ideally, your domain name too. An example is as follows:

St Mawes – friendly thatched cottage B&B. Generous Cornish breakfasts. Lovely sea views. All rooms en-suite. Prices from £35 pp. RoseCottage.co.uk. **01326 123456**

This gives readers your main selling points and contact details. Don't forget, the purpose of this kind of advert is not to tell the reader everything about you but to get them to telephone you or visit your website. They will find out the rest at that stage.

PUBLIC RELATIONS

You would not be best advised to engage a PR firm but, if you have the time and interest, you could do some PR work yourself. Write a press release about your 'third night free' offer and send it to the travel editors of all the national newspapers. You might just get a paragraph in a travel section worth many hundreds of pounds. PR is not a closed order – anyone can do it. If it costs little but might gain you a lot, it may be worth the time.

Your clients are your best salespeople!

You are missing a seam of gold if you don't have a guest book. Praise from guests is the most persuasive kind of salesmanship and better than anything you can say yourself. What marketers call 'testimonials' are nuggets of marketing gold and they are free for the asking.

Buy an attractive, hardback guest book or visitors book, with ruled pages with narrow left-hand columns for date and name/address, then a wide column for comments. As guests are leaving, invite them to write in your guest book if they would like to.

We have been constantly surprised and delighted at the lovely comments we get from guests in our guest book. Many guests also find it reassuring and interesting to read through the comments from previous guests. Our book includes comments from guests from Japan, America, Sweden, Holland, France, Canada, Hong Kong, Australia, Austria, Germany, Italy, Pakistan and Réunion Island – and, of course, from England, Scotland, Wales and Northern Ireland.

What else can you do with your guest book, other than let guests read it? Go through it regularly for quotations, and put them in your brochure, and on your website. Be careful to quote accurately, and either:

☐ ask each person whose quotation you use whether you can reproduce it – if you have their permission, you can attribute their quotation by name; or

☐ reproduce the quotes on an unattributable basis.

As the first is logistically difficult, we recommend the second: simply attribute the quotation to 'Mrs B of Cheltenham', or 'Mr S of Buenos Aires, Argentina', or even just 'a guest from Cape Town, South Africa, June 2005'.

18
ONLINE MARKETING

The importance of online marketing

Online advertising is getting more and more important all the time, as everyone now realises. If you are not interested in computers and are tempted to ignore online marketing because it is an unknown or baffling area, we have one word of advice: don't! The advantages and effectiveness of online advertising just cannot be ignored, and if you do things properly (not as difficult as you might think) you may, like us, find that most of your B&B business comes from your online advertising.

The great advantage of the Internet is that it has levelled the playing field to some extent between small businesses like B&Bs and very large ones like international hotel chains. Just five to ten years ago, a small B&B would not have a hope of rivalling a hotel chain in its advertising efforts, particularly in international advertising. The big chains could afford to spend huge amounts of money on advertising campaigns in many different countries, which would generate them business from abroad and from within the UK, whereas a small B&B could not hope to do more than get a listing in the local tourist office brochure or (at the cost of a large percentage of commission on every booking) in a tour operator's brochure.

 Set up a simple but effective website and promote it to search engines. Use keyword advertising. You don't have to spend much, but do spend it wisely.

Now that has all changed: your B&B can have a website as effective as that of any chain hotel, and it is within your grasp to ensure that, if someone from Saskatchewan, Smolensk or Sydney (or, if it comes to that, Surbiton) is planning to visit your area, they are as likely to find information about your B&B as about the nearest Hilton or Travelodge. And business gained this way is direct business – there is no middleman to pay commission to!

International business is especially attractive because:

    ☐   tourists from abroad are generally prepared to pay more, and add more extras, than UK residents on a domestic break; and

    ☐   they generally stay longer.

So you cannot and must not ignore the Internet. There is absolutely no reason, on cost or any other grounds, why a small B&B should not have its own website – and every reason why it should. It can be a real business generator.

Choosing a domain name

A domain name – sometimes called a URL – is just the website's address. For example, our B&B's domain name is 'www.thepheasants.com'. It is becoming standard now to omit the 'www'. In promotional literature and on letterheads, we simply say 'thepheasants.com'.

Domain names can easily be registered for under £10. At Hostway.co.uk, for example, '.co.uk' domain names cost £7.95 for two years, and '.com' domain names cost £15.95 for two years. You can only register a domain name if it is available – that is, if nobody else has registered it yet. This is getting harder all the time as so many good names have been used. If you are unlucky, you may find that someone has registered the name you want so that, instead of being able to register it new for under £10, you may have to make a substantial offer to an Internet name broker.

What domain name should you choose? The best one is the name of your B&B, followed by '.com' or '.co.uk', especially if your B&B's spelling is obvious. Adding the name of the town may be a good idea too. For example 'rosecottage.co.uk' or 'rosecottageamberley.co.uk' would be good names.

Points to bear in mind are as follows:

☐ Avoid very long domain names.

☐ Avoid difficult spellings if you can.

☐ You can't use '&' in a domain name – so 'b&b' would have to be 'bandb'.

☐ Avoid hyphens: use 'rosecottage.com' rather than 'rose-cottage.com'.

☐ '.com' is probably best, followed by '.co.uk'. You are best advised not to use other suffixes (e.g. '.info', '.biz' etc.) in your domain name as these are not the obvious ones, so people may not find you.

☐ Avoid text-speak (e.g. 'rosecottage4u.com'). Again it is not obvious, so may not be found and does not give a professional image.

Once you have registered a domain name, you can upload a website to that domain and then your site will be live on the World Wide Web and can be viewed by anyone on the planet! Uploading your site is technical and outside the scope of this book, but is fairly simple with free FTP (File Transfer Protocol) software like CuteFTP from Globalscape. Your website hosting company will be able to guide you through all the steps required.

Using a website template

You can put together a very simple, one-page website using Word software. We did this and it worked well for our first year or more. For a much more professional-looking website, you can use website templates which can be bought online from under $100, and then you can put your own words and pictures on them. These web templates give you a professional look and feel with headers, menu structures and forms which you would not be able to create yourself without advanced skills in HTML, the web developer's programming language. Our current website for The Pheasants was home made this way and it gets a lot of compliments from guests (see www.thepheasants.com).

Our website at www.howtorunabandb.com has more detail on this and links to various sources of website templates. You can adapt the templates to your own website relatively simply with basic computer skills, patience – and time!

TEN WEBSITE DOS

• **Do** make sure your homepage gives a clear message of exactly what you are offering, how to find out more and how to book. (Sorry if this sounds basic, but I am constantly being amazed by sites – even of large and prestigious companies who have clearly spent a lot of money on their site – who have forgotten to make clear exactly what they are offering and to whom.)

• **Do** think about your site from your client's point of view: what are they looking for, what will attract them and are you giving it to them?

• **Do** make clear you are selling something, exactly what, exactly how to book and at what price.

• **Do** 'layer' information intelligently: concise and punchy on your homepage, with clear links to more detailed pages for those who are eager for information (and don't forget, as even the fustiest museum knows, to 'lead them out via the shop').

• **Do** remember that the Internet is primarily a *reading* medium and your readers are looking for specific content to read. Unless you are selling pictures, your site's images should add to and support your words, not be used for cheap decoration. So many sites take up lots of space with bought-in stock photos which look pretty but are irrelevant or confusing to the message.

• **Do** keep your site simple. Remember its purpose: just because you can add a gimmick (and you always can), it does not mean that you should.

• **Do** keep checking your search-engine ranking by doing searches and seeing where you come – and let your web people know if you are not happy with the results!

• **Do** get unbiased, critical people whose judgement you trust to look at your site and tell you honestly what they think. And be brave – and grateful!

• **Do** think about the most likely search words your chosen audience would use, and ensure your site's 'meta-tags' are based on these (your web designer will know the technicalities). If your clients are searching for 'cheap rooms', don't use 'inexpensive accommodation'.

• **Do** promote your site with a well planned e marketing campaign. Just having a great store is no good if nobody enters!

TEN WEBSITE DON'TS

• **Don't** sign up with a company offering automatically to submit your site to hundreds of search engines. Most of these are so-called 'link farms' and using them may actually harm your search-engine ranking with the major search engines.

• **Don't** be tempted to indulge in a slick, 'flash' animation page before your homepage. Most people skip them, they slow down websurfers with a dialup connection and they can hide your site from search engines, so reducing your ranking.

• **Don't** use small, unreadable type, put type over images or 'reverse' type in white out of a dark background: all these actively discourage readership.

• **Don't** waffle, overuse clichés or pad out your words: use concise, readable and relevant words, to convey your message with clarity.

• **Don't** let web designers or agencies confuse you or blind you with science. Make sure their work is simply enabling and reinforcing your powerful sales message. Science should follow salesmanship, not the other way round!

• **Don't** shout when I'm right next to you. Don't fill your site with neon colours, flashing banners, animation and exclamation marks. Once your reader is there, the attention-seeking can stop: they want content.

• **Don't** talk about yourself and your business; talk about your client and the benefits you can offer them.

• **Don't** try to give your site mass appeal if you are after a tiny band of enthusiasts or cognoscenti – there is no value in alienating your buyers by attracting non-buyers. Focus on your purpose!

• **Don't** boast, make overblown claims or exaggerate. Your readers are intelligent, remember – just like you.

• **Don't** use slang, bad grammar or mis-spellings. Your readers will not want to do business with you if you lose their respect.

Finally, discuss your requirements with a sensible and knowledgeable web enabler, but never forget: you are their client, and salesmanship must come before science!

Search engines – the 'Google' effect

As we all know, there has been a revolution on how people typically look for information in the last few years – mainly just in the last three to five years, in fact. This is the 'Google' effect. It has shaken up the travel and tourism industry particularly.

What the revolution has meant is that, if you or I want to find out something, one of the main ways we will do so – perhaps the first choice for most – is using an Internet search engine, which in practice means *the* Internet search engine, Google. As a result Google has arguably become the most successful new business in the history of the world, and it is still only eight years old. All this means that, today, and even more so in the future and especially for younger people, the way your potential customers will search for their B&B accommodation is by typing a few words into Google.

 Sleep in each guest room occasionally and look at it critically from a guest's point of view, paying attention to every detail. You can then make improvements before having to react to complaints.

This is both good and bad news for you. The good news is that this levels the playing field to a large extent for small B&Bs by taking away much of the marketing advantage the big hotel groups had in the past with their big advertising budgets. A small B&B can do as well in a Google search as a Hilton or Marriott. More good news is that this does not have to be expensive and may well be cheaper for the same result than old-fashioned print advertising. More good news is that it is instant and flexible. You don't have to wait until the next issue is published to run an ad or to change your wording.

And the bad news? Everyone else is trying to do the same, too, so you have a lot of competition for that all-important Google search result ranking.

HOW TO USE GOOGLE

There are two aspects to Google:

☐ The search listings, which appear in the centre of the screen.

☐ The 'sponsored links' or paid-for search results listed at the top in a tint box and down the right-hand side of the screen.

Your position in the search listings is ultimately outside your control because it is based on Google's editorial policy as executed by its very sophisticated software and indexing systems. However you can and should do a few key things to give your site the best chance of a good ranking. This book would need to be twice as long to do justice to this subject, but here are a few brief pointers:

☐ Work out what words and phrases your potential customers are most likely to be searching on (try asking a few!). These keywords are the basis of your Google success. They might include 'St Mawes B&Bs', 'St Mawes accommodation', 'hotels St Mawes', 'Cornwall B&B', etc.

☐ Title every page of your website clearly, including with these search keywords.

☐ Make sure the content of your homepage – the text – contains as many relevant words and phrases as possible, including alternative combinations of your location and 'B&B', 'accommodation', 'bed and breakfast' etc., and lots of relevant description, and including your top keywords.

☐ Make sure every picture has a relevant caption as 'alternative text' (this is part of HTML code), and that at least one has your B&B name and location as its caption – e.g. 'Rose Cottage B&B, St Mawes, Cornwall, UK'.

☐ Use the meta-tag descriptions within the HTML code for each web page (apologies for all this jargon, and this is getting too detailed and technical for this book, but the help from your hosting company or website template will explain).

☐ Submit your homepage to Google manually at google.com/addurl.

☐ Get as many other websites as possible (and, ideally, popular and relevant ones) to add a link to your website.

☐ Make your domain name relevant to searches where possible (that is a reason for including the resort name within the domain name).

This is not always an exact science, and submitting your website can take several days to take effect, but keep doing searches and seeing where you come in the listings, and try to work out how you can improve your ranking.

GOOGLE 'ADWORDS' ADVERTISING

The above was all about getting better rankings in Google's free search listings. As we said at the start, though, you also have another bite at the cherry, and this one is in your control – but it costs money! This is paid-for 'cost per click' advertising, or what Google calls its 'AdWords' program.

Basically, this is very simple. You pay a set amount for every click – i.e. every time an Internet user sees your Google sponsored link (ad) and clicks through to your website. Which Internet users are shown your ads is determined by keywords you set and how closely these correspond to the search word or phrase that Internet user has Googled, and also by the budget you have set.

For example, you could pay for the keywords 'St Mawes B&B'. Every time an Internet user anywhere in the world (you can limit it to certain countries if you want) types 'St Mawes B&B' into Google, your ad should be shown alongside the search results – provided your budget is sufficient.

Your budget determines not only whether your ad is shown but also in what ranking it is shown compared with other ads. If it is not on the first page, it is vastly less likely to be seen and clicked on, and if after the second page it becomes vanishingly unlikely to be clicked on.

Be methodical to the point of obsession about accurate and up-to-date record keeping – especially your bookings book! A small slip can cause you huge problems.

This is all about relevance, so the more specific you can be, the more relevant you can be. And if you are in a very small location or are the only B&B there, you have a big advantage in that no competitors will also be paying for that location as a keyword.

There are hundreds of B&Bs in Blackpool so, if you are in Blackpool, you are very unlikely to get listed very near the top of a search for 'Blackpool B&B'. However, if you are the only B&B in Nethercombe Lacy village, you are 100% certain to come top of anyone's search for 'Nethercombe Lacy B&B'.

Again, AdWords could (and has) merited a book in itself, so we have confined ourselves to the basic principles so that you can plan your online promotion via Google, and to this word of advice: don't ignore Google, embrace it!

To get started, go to google.co.uk/ads. You'll find it very easy.

PART THREE
WHAT NEXT?

19
EXPANDING YOUR BUSINESS

Adding extras

Although your main focus must always be on your strengths and your core business – the B&B – it is a good habit in any business, once it is up and running, to look for ways in which you can generate additional revenue over and above the main income stream. As long as this additional income does not compromise your main business in any way and does not require disproportionate effort or management time, it is 'incremental' income which can help to maximise the return on your asset – the property you are running as a B&B.

The key principles are:

☐ keep it simple: don't invent complex new businesses; and

☐ make sure the 'add on' business reinforces and complements your basic B&B business, rather than distracts from it.

Here your choices depend on the nature of the B&B you are running and its target market, on the local area, and on your own skills, experience and interests.

SERVING DRINKS AND MEALS

We have chosen to become licensed and to sell wines by the glass and bottle. If every guest had one glass of wine every night, that would increase our sales by 11.2% (a glass sells at £3.70, so two are £7.40 against our double-room rate of £66). At the time of writing, a guest has just checked out having stayed for two nights and having spent about £70 in bar bills on top of his accommodation costs. The gross profit on this is at least 60%.

As you can see, this has the potential of being an excellent new revenue stream – and one that is very complementary to the B&B accommodation business (see Chapter 8 for full details about how to become licensed). Another big area of add-on sales is of course meals. We have dealt with these in Chapter 13.

GUIDED WALKS AND THEMED BREAKS

Besides drinks and meals, there are other things you can do to gain extra revenue. Some B&B owners offer guided walks locally for a charge, especially if they happen to be trained Blue Badge guides.

Others use their own interests to create themed breaks for guests, which then sell for more than their standard room rate. These vary from bridge classes to flower arranging to wine appreciation (if you are licensed!) to history to arts and crafts – there is no limit to the subjects. The point is that you can add value with a theme, event or masterclass and make what you are offering unique into the bargain. It does not have to be your own speciality: you can work with a local expert to set up themed breaks based at your B&B.

Growing your business

When your business is up and running and you have got to grips with the problems and know how to make the profits flow, you will want to expand the business. This is where a B&B business is at a disadvantage compared with other types of business. If you make Mars bars, you can easily manufacture more to meet demand, but a B&B business is a prisoner of its physical property. Your turnover is limited by the number of rooms you have and the number of days in the year.

ADDING MORE ROOMS

What you may be able to do, if successful, is raise your prices and thus increase turnover and profits. You may also be able to add another room or two, either by converting another part of the building or by adding an extension – or even by building an annexe if you have room on your land.

You will be able to judge the economics of this by comparing building quotes with what you would be likely to make in revenue from the extra space over the next few years. Don't forget that, with property, you also get an added bonus from capital appreciation over time, which helps tip the balance in favour of development.

BUYING ANOTHER PROPERTY

Another route to expansion once you have a successful business model and an ever-increasing flow of customers is to duplicate: buy another property and operate it as a B&B. This could be a separately operated business, but gaining your flow of customers and your overall management (perhaps run day-to-day by an employee manager), or effectively an expansion of your business – for instance, perhaps the property next door could be bought and connected?

If your property itself is not your unique selling point, and your success is from your own quality of service, marketing and hard work, then you have another option: sell up and buy a bigger property with more rooms instead.

Be creative – there are always ways you can scale up a successful business.

20
SELLING YOUR BUSINESS

There may come a time when you will want to sell your B&B, so this book would be incomplete without covering the selling process – or at least preparations for a sale.

Deciding to sell

Selling is not failure. It is simply part of any planned business cycle. There comes a time when your life's priorities mean that the reasons for selling (releasing cash, downsizing your property, cutting your workload or relocation) outweigh the reasons for carrying on as you are.

Your reasons for selling are very relevant, both to how you plan the sale and to the buyer, who will always want to know. Yes, you may think it is none of their business but, if you want to make your sale as easy and as successful as possible, you will understand your buyer's reasons for wanting to know yours and develop a very well argued explanation to give.

As we said earlier, because most B&Bs are basically private houses, their sale will follow the dictates of the housing market in almost all respects. In most cases, the B&B will be valued as a house, with some additional value to represent its earning potential as a business. However, this would only be relevant to buyers who intend to carry on your B&B business. You may find that many buyers will only be interested in the property as a home. As this book is about B&Bs, we will assume that you are offering the property for sale as a B&B and that it will be bought as a B&B.

Planning the sale

Just as we insisted on the importance of planning ahead carefully before you started your B&B, we now want to emphasise how important early planning is to a sale. The worst situation to be in is to have to sell in a hurry.

So think ahead, well *before* anything happens in your life which may force a decision.

Here are a few things to consider:

☐ Property prices: try not to sell at the bottom of a property depression!

☐ Seasonal timing: perhaps not quite as important as it used to be, but the best times to go to market are still spring and late summer/autumn, and it is still best to avoid midwinter or the high summer holiday period.

☐ Your B&B accounts: the best value will be obtained from a good succession of steadily growing revenue figures. If the current season will be much better than last, it may be better to time the sale so that this can show up in a set of comparative accounts. If, however, this season looks like being a downturn, perhaps you should sell now and use the results to date in your marketing.

☐ Get very early advice (it cannot ever be too early) from experienced local estate agents about the likely demand for your property. Don't forget, they may advise that it would sell best as a home. In that case many months of future bookings would actually be a negative which might deter buyers. It is always better to hear such advice, weigh it up and decide what to do about it than to decide not to listen because it may not be what you wanted to hear.

☐ This early estate agency advice will also help in identifying enhancements you should make pre-sale: those things which will add more value than they cost and which will attract buyers and speed the sale process. It may be worth decorating tired or unfashionably decorated rooms, painting the outside of the house or trimming lawns and hedges and filling the flowerbeds with new blooms. First impressions to visitors are very important to a sale.

☐ These improvements must also be photographed, and you must use your very best pictures for the sales literature (blue sky and flowers make any external shot more attractive than leaden winter skies and bare trees).

☐ Make sure your leaflet, stationery and website look as good as you can make them, as they will be the first thing that most potential buyers will see.

☐ Think about how the selling process will affect B&B guests. It may not be a good idea, for instance, to let the estate agent put a For Sale board outside because people are less likely to book ahead at a B&B they know is for sale. This is another area where running a B&B is a complication to the usual property sale process.

It seems obvious, but a business (like anything else) is only worth what you can get a buyer to pay for it.

So you will never actually know the true value of your business until you start getting firm bids, and ultimately until you sell it. However, different types of business have their own widely recognised yardsticks for valuation and, while by no means foolproof, these are useful. When you start to think ahead towards selling your B&B, you should certainly look at these yardsticks, as they are the best means you have of gauging the likely value of your B&B.

Valuing your business

The best financial valuation of any business is in relation to its sustainable profitability and return on investment. 'Sustainable' means the ongoing level of profitability which a new owner could rely upon given a realistic trading forecast based on established patterns, and having allowed for any anomalies the current owner may have injected in the profit and loss figures.

For example, if you have always done all the cleaning and laundry yourself, this will have kept your costs down and flattered your profit figures, but a prospective owner may feel this is unsustainable and allow for higher future costs in cleaners and laundry bills, and therefore lower sustainable profits.

Conversely (and this would help your sales pitch), if you have always farmed out the laundry and cleaning at great expense, you could point out how much a new owner with more time could add to the sustainable profits by doing these things in-house.

A widely used method of valuing businesses is a 'price-to-earnings ratio' (p/e ratio). Different business sectors have different p/e ratios, which in the case of sectors featured on the stock exchange are easy to find. If shares in a particular sector tend to be valued at, say, six times earnings, then roughly speaking a business in that sector is worth six times its earnings (i.e. its sustainable profits), all else being equal.

It would be nice to be able to quote a p/e ratio for B&Bs but, unfortunately, for very small property-based businesses, the other variables (location, condition, property valuation, the state of the property market, interest rates, etc.) are so important that any such figure would be meaningless.

Trading figures

This sustainability concept also shows how important a well documented record of trading figures is. Where a business has just started, and valuation will be based on hope or wishful thinking, but where there is a solid record of sales, the valuation can be solid, too.

And because businesses are valued on future expectations of sustainable profits, a record of steadily growing sales and profits will greatly improve the valuation of that business (just as a record of decline will greatly reduce it).

Private home or B&B?

A hospitality business like a B&B has an added complication, which is that it is not just a business but also a property. Whereas its value as a business is limited to an accepted multiple of its sustainable (or possible future) earnings in revenue from its letting rooms, your property's value may well be higher as a private home on the property market.

The UK has some of the world's highest property values, and historic features, views or a lovely setting may make less difference to what you can charge B&B guests than it does to its property value as a house.

Capital gains tax (CGT)

This hugely complex subject is outside the remit of this book and is one where you will need individual professional advice. We do want to flag up the possibility, however, that there are circumstances in which the HMRC may apply CGT on the sale of your property, even if it is primarily your family home.

If your B&B is also your family home (or has been at some time during your ownership), you will be entitled to exemption from CGT for any gain arising from the disposal of your home (principal private residence relief). However the exemption does *not* cover any part of the gain relating to part of the property used *exclusively* for 'business' (e.g. B&B) purposes.

This is a changing area, as the new Coalition government made changes to CGT in its first budget. The Bed and Breakfast Association provided its members with a detailed analysis of CGT on B&Bs, and will update it as the rules and guidelines become clearer. In the mean time, be aware of the possibility, and get professional advice based on your own individual business and personal financial circumstances.

WEBSITES

HowtoRunaBandB.com

This is the website run by the authors of this book which, besides selling the book, also has updates, further links and resources.

The Bed and Breakfast Association (BBA)

The BBA is the UK trade association for B&B and guest house owners. Its Chief Executive is David Weston, one of the authors of this book.

In July 2010 the BBA won the official accolade (through the government/CBI Trade Association Forum) of being judged the best trade association in Britain at representing its members and sector, out of 313 trade associations across all areas of activity.

The BBA has the following objectives:

1. To represent the interests of 'bed and breakfast' owners in the UK, and to campaign on behalf of those interests (for example, to government and regulatory bodies).

2. To provide information and support services to 'bed and breakfast' owners in the UK, to enable them to improve and develop their businesses.

3. To facilitate and enable the continuous professional development of the independent bed and breakfast sector in the UK, and promote best practice.

4. To promote to the public the advantages of staying in independent 'bed and breakfast' accommodation.

Membership is open to those at the planning/buying stage, as well as those running established businesses. The association is there to inform, support and represent its members.

The association's website is at: www.bandbassociation.org

The BIIAB

BIIAB (the awarding body of the British Institute of Innkeepers) is the leading awarding body for the licensed retail sector. It specialises in developing and awarding qualifications to support the industry at all levels. The BIIAB has launched the BIIAB Level 2 National Certificate for Personal Licence Holders, to coincide with the requirement of the 2003 Licensing Act which states that anyone authorising the retail sale of alcohol will have to hold a personal licence. In order to qualify for a personal licence, an applicant must hold a relevant licensing qualification such as this.

Website: www.biiab.org

INDEX

Visit our How To website at **www.howto.co.uk**

At **www.howto.co.uk** you can engage in conversation with our authors – all of whom have 'been there and done that' in their specialist fields. You can get access to special offers and additional content but, most importantly, you will be able to engage with, and become a part of, a wide and growing community of people just like yourself.

At **www.howto.co.uk** you'll be able to talk and share tips with people who have similar interests and are facing similar challenges in their lives. People who, just like you, have the desire to change their lives for the better – be it through moving to a new country, starting a new business, growing their own vegetables, or writing a novel.

At **www.howto.co.uk** you'll find the support and encouragement you need to help make your aspirations a reality.

How To Books strives to present authentic, inspiring, practical information in their books. Now, when you buy a title from **How To Books**, you get even more than just words on a page.

Printed in Great Britain
by Amazon

85748424R00113